Make and Furnish Your Own Miniature Rooms

Make and Furnish Your Own Miniature Rooms

by Marian Maeve O'Brien

Photographs by Sam Taylor

Drawings by Nancy Ovedovitz

GREENWICH HOUSE
New York

Copyright © 1976 by Marian Maeve O'Brien.

All rights reserved, including the right to reproduce this book or portions thereof in any form, except for the inclusion of brief quotations in a review.

This 1982 edition is published by Greenwich House, a division of Arlington House, Inc., distributed by Crown Publishers, Inc., by arrangement with Hawthorn Properties (E.P. Dutton, Inc.)

Manufactured in the United States of America

Library of Congress Cataloging in Publication Data

O'Brien, Marian Maeve.
    Make and furnish your own miniature rooms.

    Reprint. Originally published: New York : Hawthorn Books, c1976.
    Includes index.
    1. Miniature craft.   2. Miniature rooms.   I. Title.
[TT178.027   1982]   747′.0228   82-6038
                                            AACR2
ISBN: 0-517-383357

h g f e d c b a

To my editor,
Elizabeth Backman,
who pulled it all together

Nothing else matches the exhilaration of helping to conceive, plan and create something that has no purpose other than to give people pleasure. . . .

—Richard Rodgers
Musical Stages: An Autobiography

Contents

16 pages of color photos follow page 86

Make and Furnish Your Own Miniature Rooms

Introduction

This is a book of ideas.

I could no more tell you, in such a book, exactly how to build and furnish a certain miniature room than I could tell you how to furnish your own living room. Many things must be considered, such as your own tastes, what is available to you, what you wish to accomplish, and much more. And a book written expressly to tell you how to make and furnish a certain miniature room would be dull reading anyhow.

But there *is* a wealth of ideas here. Ideas that will spark your interest and lead you into doing something you have never done before. Something that will bring pleasure to many people and to you, too. Ideas that may be used to bring to life remembered moments of the past. Ideas that will celebrate moments of history that ring with challenge and triumph, done in your own inimitable style. Ideas that will perpetuate certain scenes, beautiful places that you want to pass on to your children.

Perhaps the oldest miniature rooms are those seen in the Metropolitan Museum of Art. They were found in the tomb of an ancient king, where they had been placed to serve his needs after he achieved immortality: a weaver shop, a carpenter's shop, a bakery, and much more were found at Thebes, but there is little that can be proven about their dates or builders.

During the seventeenth and eighteenth centuries, miniature rooms began to appear in the shape of the then ubiquitous Nuremberg kitchens, which Flora Gill Jacobs writes about in her book, *A History of Dolls' Houses*. However, between the time of the Egyptian monarchs, who presumably were buried with their favorite rooms so the royal spirits could enjoy themselves in their accustomed surroundings, and the Nuremberg kitchens and miniature rooms built for the Bourbons, there is little documented evidence about this fascinating hobby.

Molly Heikes of Durango, Colorado, sparks our imagination with a fascinating story. She has sent photos of a tiny room made of stone, which was found in 1974 by the Chaco Canyon Research Center survey crew. This was quite a distance from the visitor's area, Molly reports, and was in a side canyon that branches off the main wash; it was built under an overhanging ledge on a surface about 4' above the ground.

This room, or house, measures about 18" long and 12" high. It has only one opening—the front doorway. The entire structure is of stone, and each block has been carefully shaped so that it fits against its neighbors. When one lifts off one of the larger stones that make up the roof, one finds twigs laid across that have been placed there as roof beams, or *vigas* as they are known in the Southwest. There is even a little stone lintel over the doorway.

Archeologists called by the survey crew suggested that the structure may have been about one hundred years old and might have been made by a Navajo; there were ruins of a Navajo hogan below the ledge that hid the room. However, since it is impossible to date stone and difficult to date wood, the scientists wouldn't commit themselves to a specific date. Molly goes on to tell us that some of the survey crew, well versed in the history of this part of the country, estimated that it might have been made by an Anasazi Indian some seven or eight hundred years ago; some pieces of broken Anasazi pottery, very tiny, were found on the floor. If this estimate is correct, then this is surely one of the oldest miniature rooms yet found, with the exception of some of the early European crèches and the Egyptian rooms.

Mrs. Jacobs, again in her *History of Dolls' Houses*, salutes the Nuremberg kitchens of collector's fame and mentions a "toy kitchen made of bronze and Dresden china. . . . the saucepans are decorated with floral wreaths and the little chicken on the spit is an exquisite bit of Dresden china."

Miniature rooms picturing butcher shops were for some reason very popular in Victoria's time. We have one resplendent with gory red flesh and creamy fat. Milliner's shops also enjoyed a certain vogue; the needlework shop pictured in my book *Make Your Own Dollhouses and Dollhouse Miniatures* is another example, a kind of stall that was widely used.

Many historians suggest that the crèche may have been the origin of the miniature room. There are many beautiful ones from the seventeenth and eighteenth centuries that indicate that much skill and love were put into their building. It is largely a question of choosing a tale that suits us and going on from there.

Sufficient for our purpose is the fact that miniature rooms and shadow boxes are once again wildly popular, probably due to our generally smaller living quarters, which simply cannot accommodate the large old dollhouses, but also to the fact that we moderns have discovered the exquisite pleasure of creating one beautiful thing.

There is a tremendous excitement in building a shadow box of exactly the size we want, being able to get our hands inside it and furnish it beautifully. Access is easy when one is confronted only by three walls and a floor. A particular scene may be depicted, much as the French did in the times of the Bourbons, when lying-in rooms, praying rooms, and even the settings for murder were all favorite subjects. Lighting is very simple since each room may be lighted as though it were a tiny stage, which, of course, it is.

A miniature room may be an ornament upon a table, or it may be made in a bookcase. It may fill the empty shell of a television cabinet, or we may hang it upon a wall. We can take it with us when we go, with none of the moving problems presented by large dollhouses, which often seem to be more difficult to move than full-size households.

Your miniature room will, indeed, open a whole new world of miniature planning to you. If this idea enthralls you as it has many, that's all to the good, for with it you have no limitations. A dollhouse can hold your treasures only to the extent enclosed by its four walls, but you can always build another room and create another beautiful picture. That, to me, has proven to be the ultimate satisfaction while creating my own series of rooms.

PART I

1 Works of the Masters

The one great inspiration for miniature rooms in America was developed during the 1930s and 1940s by the late Mrs. James Ward Thorne of Chicago, Illinois.

As a child Narcissa Thorne had loved dollhouses, as a young girl she had collected eighteenth-century "sample" furniture, and as an adult traveler she had searched the shops of the United States and Europe for antique miniatures. By 1930 she had acquired an enormous quantity of furniture and accessories, all in the $\frac{1}{12}$ scale, plus many remnants of cloth with tiny prints or patterns. She decided that her treasures could most effectively be displayed in a series of rooms built to the same scale as the miniatures: 1″ to 1′.

We are told in a catalogue, *Thorne Miniature Rooms* by Betsey B. Creekmore from the Dulin Gallery of Art that Mrs. Thorne borrowed the idea of the diorama, a miniature scene in a shallow, glass-fronted box that was hung on the wall at adult eye level from European museums. By deepening her rooms and recessing them into the wall, she was able to invent an entirely new technique of concealed illumination for them; light came through windows and doors as it does in adult-size houses. Carrying this idea a step further, she arranged street scenes or gardens outside the lighted windows to be seen through their glass. As she elaborated on this technique, tantalizing glimpses of adjoining rooms appeared through archways or open doors.

Adding to her already extensive knowledge of history and architecture by intensive research, Mrs. Thorne planned twenty-eight period rooms, drawing a detailed sketch of each room for the cabinetmaker chosen to construct them. She then painted or stained the woodwork, papered the walls, made curtains and carpets, and upholstered the furniture.

Even with so large a collection upon which to draw, there were gaps in the furnishings of each room. Mrs. Thorne commissioned small-

This Old Curiosity Shop is the favorite miniature room of John Stover's collection. The authentic Breton farmhouse interior, with Williamsburg blue and white woodwork and dado and pink and white scenic wallpaper, was made by Eugene Kupjack for Narcissa Thorne.

scale copies of selected museum pieces, and these reproductions fitted in so happily with her genuine antiques that it is impossible to distinguish the old from the new. Ingenuity guided her use of everyday objects in the same unusual ways that we have stressed in this series of books: handkerchiefs became curtains; petit-point handbags and box tops masqueraded as area rugs; seals and chessmen turned into portrait busts and statuettes; minuscule candles were made in a dozen different ways.

In 1937 she presented a group of twenty-nine rooms to the Art Institute of Chicago, tracing the development of styles in England and France from 1500 to the 1920s, and in 1942 she added a third and final group so that the Art Institute could point with pride to a doll's-eye

Narcissa Thorne made this Victorian living room for John Stover in 1962. The palm in the corner and the whatnot shelf were added later. The ceramic pieces were made by Frieda Leininger. The 1″ stereoscope has double cards printed in color and actually works.

view of American history from 1675 to 1940. It was at this time that I became acquainted with her through an interview, and we became fast friends for the remainder of her life.

Mrs. Thorne's solution of the problem of scale in these rooms is almost magical. While recognizing that an absolute solution is hardly possible, she has succeeded to an unprecedented degree in relating each part so that a feeling of complete consistency has been attained. Special processes were developed for obtaining a hairline fineness in moldings and ornament, and even the textiles were specially prepared in many instances to give the faery delicacy that was demanded.

Today, many of the conditions that seemed insurmountable to Mrs. Thorne are taken care of for you and me. New glues make it possible to hang wallpaper and affix woodwork with a minimum of exasperation. Much woodwork can be found already shaped and sanded, so that only painting is needed. And while we may not be able to travel the world in search of certain pieces as Mrs. Thorne did, we have innumerable accomplished artists in the field of miniatures, whose fine pieces we can use to augment our own efforts or to complete our furnished rooms entirely, so that whether we are reproducing a period, depicting an event, or merely furnishing a showcase for fine pieces we've acquired, our box rooms can indeed be a source of satisfaction and a joy even to our heirs.

So many beautiful rooms are being produced today that it's a bit risky to name names; however, John and Ellen Blauer of San Francisco are so outstanding that there could be no quarrel with their heading the list. Illustrations of many of their works will be found in this book.

Another builder of miniature rooms of absolute perfection is Tom Devereaux of Chicago. His are made in boxes with picture-frame fronts that show off his beautiful details perfectly. Except for a few pieces made by invitation specifically for these rooms, Devereaux makes everything himself: carpets, draperies, furniture, chandeliers, all the rest. Thus, he is accomplishing through his own efforts the results that Mrs. Thorne was able to accomplish only by using a small army of artists. Since each room takes many hundreds of hours to complete, the cost is in direct proportion to the hours invested, which puts a Devereaux box or a Blauer room in a more expensive price range than most of us can afford. Another great artist in the field is Eugene Kupjack, who is known the world over for his miniature sterling silver pieces as well as for his rooms.

The Grandmother Stover room was made by Narcissa Thorne as an incentive for John Stover to start his own collection of miniature rooms. This is one of the few rooms in which a doll was utilized. The grandmother has real diamonds in her ring and necklace.

Louis XV dining room made by Tom Devereaux, one of this country's greatest miniaturists.

French salon with crystal chandelier made by Tom Devereaux.

I believe that after studying the illustrations in this book, you will feel the same satisfaction from owning miniature masterpieces as you would from acquiring a great work of art in the related areas of sculpture and painting. It follows, then, that a commensurate pleasure will come to you in doing the creating yourself.

Devereaux gives us this description of the Louis XV dining room:

"The walls are pale ivory over an ivory and gilt wainscoting, and the ceiling cornice is a very ornate gilt and ivory molding. The floor is $\frac{3}{4}'' \times \frac{3}{4}''$ black and white vinyl set in a diamond pattern to simulate the marble floors widely used in the reigns of the French kings.

The doors are quite high; door frames, floor moldings, and pillars are black marble and match the pilasters beside the French doors.

Draperies used at the French doors are a blue and silver leaf-pattern brocade shot with silver threads. The swags and cascades are lined with pale blue. The blue and old ivory Persian-design rug on the floor nearly matches the blue in the drapery fabric. The two gold-leafed cathedral-type stands each hold a five-branch Roman goddess candelabrum.

The dainty hand-decorated furniture in this room was done by Manijeh Tabrizi, a Pakistani student who was studying at the Art Institute of Chicago. The inlay work on the table (which opens), server, and sideboard is uneven but is true to the way the work was done in that period. All the ten pieces are a beautiful light walnut. All drawers, legs, and panels are outlined in a very minute, intricate design. The upholstery on the six chairs is leather but is painted to resemble needlepoint.

Over the server and cupboard, in very ornate fine gilt frames, are silk portrait copies of paintings of court ladies by Jean Marc Nattier (1685–1766). On the sideboard wall are two nine-branch candlesticks and silver serving pieces on the server and sideboard. Hand-painted Limoges plates are displayed in the china cabinet between the French doors, and the cabinet itself holds almost a complete set of very beautiful and fragile hand-painted Haviland china."

Pink roses made by Devereaux from fresh French bread are arranged in black and gold ormolu containers that sit upon the light walnut pedestals shown in the foreground.

The French salon is equally formal, with a pair of doors on the back wall that are inset to give the impression of leading to a hallway. Here, you will notice, Devereaux has abandoned the absolutely balanced plan that he used in the dining room; one alcove features a painting and the other a mirror. While the walnut fireplace with a gilt table and two chairs upholstered in needlepoint are the focus, at left he has placed a desk with chair and at right an upholstered chair with an inlaid table complete with a gold coffee set. Again, the chandelier and crystal sconces dominate the room.

At the opposite end of the scale in artistry but at the top in practicality and inventiveness is a series of three rooms that were built by the Cleveland Miniaturia Society in the summer of 1975 as a project for the Rainbow Babies and Children of the University Hospital complex in Cleveland, the home base of the CMS. The idea was suggested by the child-care director of Rainbow Hospital as a tool to dispel children's fears of the unknown. The series was to include a miniature operating room, a recovery room, and a patient's room.

First, members of the society made the trip to the hospital armed with cameras, tape measures, drawing pads, and other equipment. Since only four people were allowed in the operating room, four members donned sterile garments and observed and photographed, sketched and measured everything in the room.

Boxes for the rooms were made and sent to the chairmen of the committees in charge—one for each of the rooms and one to be responsible for the dolls. The boxes were sanded and painted with actual paint that had been used on the walls of the hospital, and tile floors were laid—made of vinyl tiles, cut ¾″ square, grouted, then covered with several coats of sealer.

All rooms were equipped with fluorescent lighting; the operating room had two large working spotlights over the table.

The doll committee went to work dressing the sets of dollhouse-size dolls—one black family and one white family, plus a man dressed as a doctor and two women dressed as nurses in white pants suits. At the second workshop on this project, another group made hickory-nut heads and pipe cleaner bodies for a black doctor, an Irish doctor with red hair, a Jewish doctor, and several nurses. The hospital furnished a surgery gown, paper shoes, and hats to use as material for the clothes.

The rooms were used as exhibits at the society's annual Miniature Fair in 1975 and then were presented to the hospital and accepted with great enthusiasm by the staff. It was planned that they would be shown to children about to go to surgery so that by playacting they could be relieved of some of their fears.

My feeling is that such a project shows true imagination. It also demonstrates the scope of the possibilities of miniature rooms once we venture beyond the usual nineteenth-century room-and-store ideas.

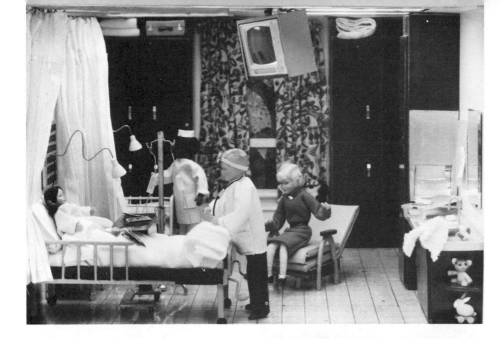

In the patient's room, everything is handmade, even the chair that reclines so that mother may nap and the overbed table with comic books on it. (*Photograph courtesy of the Cleveland Miniaturia Society*)

Cupboards in the operating room are completely equipped with all necessary items, and everything the doctor needs is at hand. Dolls include two doctors, two nurses, an anesthesiologist, and a patient. (*Photograph courtesy of the Cleveland Miniaturia Society*)

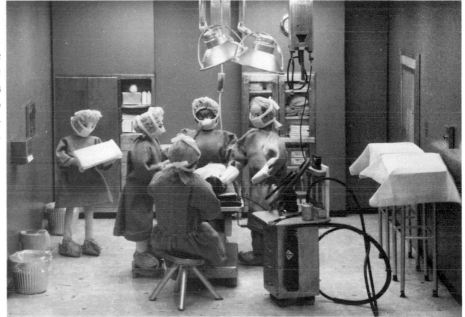

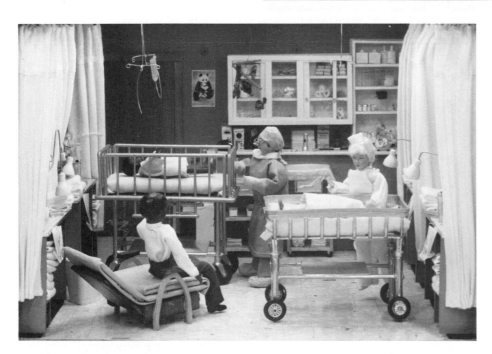

In the recovery room, a counter is fitted with flashlight, stethoscopes, and a telephone, and oxygen equipment is ready to use. The cart (left) actually rolls, so the children can move it from room to room. (*Photograph courtesy of the Cleveland Miniaturia Society*)

The Federal bedroom by Tom Devereaux is highlighted by beautiful cornices in a toile de Jouy print that is repeated on the bed and chairs.

This version of a *fin de siècle* bedroom is made almost entirely of wicker pieces by Bob Bernhard of Dolphin Originals. He also made the wing chair (rear left) and the Chinese red bombé chest (rear right). The two chests are from Petite Princess; the mirror above the one on the left dates from 1830 and has a reverse-painting panel at top. Bernhard bought the lovely glazed chintz in Barbados. The tiny slippers were made by Sylvia Rountree of the Dolls' Cobbler, and the clock (left) was made by Mary Rahrers of Sault Ste. Marie, Ontario.

2 The Versatility of Box Rooms

Probably the greatest joy that comes to us after we decide to make and treasure box rooms is the fact that they will fit into any situation. They may be large or they may be small. They may be tall and impressive or squat and homey. This is best exemplified in the group of boxes now being offered by the Sonia Messer Import Company (see page 20). These boxes give an idea of the different moldings and sizes available. The little square box at top left might be used as shown, to highlight just two fine pieces, whereas the wide box at lower left will present a picture of a whole room.

Versatility is illustrated in the next photo, which features a group of boxes made by Ron T. Muckerman, a cabinetmaker who is now making box rooms in kit form so that the collector may have the fun of achieving a finished product without too much effort.

I have long used a standard size for my box rooms just so they would be interchangeable, as illustrated on pages 24 and 25. In addition, I felt that most dollhouse rooms were too small for proper arrangement of furniture, and I wanted a size that would enable me to really present a picture without the clutter that characterizes most dollhouse rooms and that we wouldn't tolerate for a moment in our own adult-size houses.

Muckerman made my boxes 20″ wide, 12″ deep, and 11″ high out of ⅜″ plywood. For me this proved perfect, but I would strongly suggest your trying a few other sizes. Sonia Messer offers the boxes in nearly every size imaginable, from 10″ × 8″ × 6″ deep to 24″ × 12″ × 14″ deep. Some as large as 19″ wide are made only 6″ deep, but these, of course, would not provide for a room arrangement; they would merely serve as shadow boxes for showing off one or two pieces of furniture. Anyway, what you must have is what suits your purpose, so try a few in different combinations with due regard for the space in which the box must fit.

This assortment of box rooms will help you decide upon the measurements of your own. Imported by Sonia Messer, they range from the small, squarish box at top left (10″ × 8″) to the largest at bottom left (24″ × 12″). (*Photograph courtesy of Sonia Messer Imports*)

If a standard-size box is used, it may be varied by changing the location of openings and by using it horizontally or vertically. The vertical box (right) may be used as a two-storey entrance hall. Boxes by Ron Muckerman.

This authentic English-pub kit is marketed by Craft Patterns (see Appendix) and is about 15″ wide. The fire in the fireplace glows, the Christmas tree lights up, and the lantern and sconce also light.

For the builder who doesn't care to start from scratch, rooms such as this one are perfect. Marketed in kit form from Craft Patterns, it is finished with clapboarding. The dimensions are 15″ wide, 8″ deep, and 13½″ to the roof peak.

This box room with a porch was originally built in 1905. It was recently restored by Louise Bradley for the St. Joseph, Missouri, Doll Museum. It is painted in shocking pink with white trim and has a slate blue roof. (*Photograph by Nal Lawhon*)

With box rooms one is not limited to arranging the miniature rooms on shelves or standing upon a table. If you have space, you might arrange a whole house in various configurations as shown in figures 1 and 2, so that your miniature family has a constant change of scene!

Consider, for example, Arrangement A, in which we look down on the floor plan of a box arrangement. Small arrows indicate the front of the boxes, and the combination of square and oblong rooms makes for an interesting arrangement. In this, as in the other arrangements pictured, box rooms are used to actually make a dollhouse, but one that might be picked up and carried at your convenience, set up for a special event, or changed around as the spirit moves you. The only requirement here is that you have a table large enough to accommodate the one-storey house, which is about 48″ wide and 36″ deep and has open ends of the rooms on all sides.

With less space, you might prefer Arrangement B, and here the arrows indicate a one-storey arrangement, but consider the possibilities if you use it as a front elevation with the boxes piled atop each other for a three-storey house! It happens that in this arrangement we used only square boxes, 12″ × 12″, but these could be readily enlarged.

The device of a wall jutting into a room is used to show a scene outside the window. (*Photograph by Philip Weibler, courtesy of Carlson's Miniatures*)

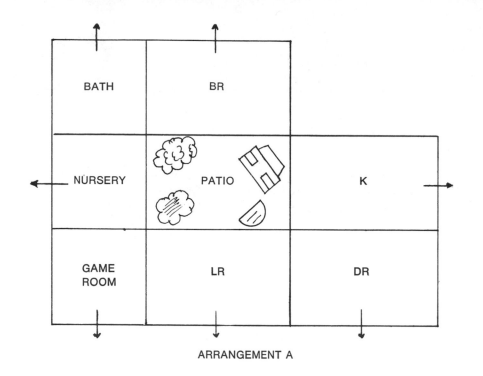

Figure 1

BATH	BR	
NURSERY	PATIO	K
GAME ROOM	LR	DR

ARRANGEMENT A

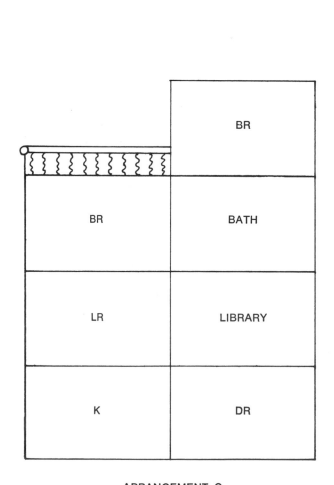

BR	
BR	BATH
LR	LIBRARY
K	DR

ARRANGEMENT C

			BR
		BR	BATH
K	DR	LR	GARAGE

ARRANGEMENT B

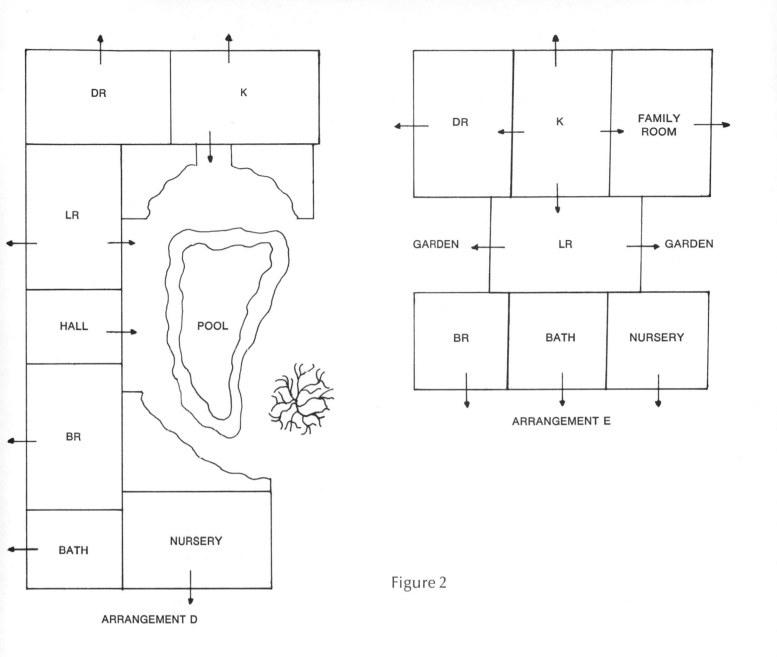

ARRANGEMENT D

ARRANGEMENT E

ARRANGEMENT F

Figure 2

Another possibility is Arrangement C, which is only 36″ wide but four storeys high. Here, again, all of the rooms face front so that your treasures are readily accessible. Note how the little railing atop the lower roof provides a sun deck or roof terrace for the family.

Arrangement D is much more elaborate and requires much more space, but laid out on a ping-pong table or a similar area, you can have a great deal of fun, not only displaying your finest pieces, but arranging the gardens, trees, and pools. Here, again, we use a combination of square and oblong boxes for added interest, some of them with open sides toward the garden, some open to the outside, and the living room with a look-through arrangement of two entrances.

Arrangement E also makes provision for a garden. Notice here that one wing of the house is made up of square, small rooms, and the other is interesting because it uses larger oblong rooms. In this case, again, the living room is the hub of the house with entrances from three sides, and all other rooms open to the outside.

Arrangement F is another front elevation of a two-storey house. While I consider this a most elegant design because all rooms are reached from the front, notice that it will take some 5½′ of space.

It is possible to start with just a few boxes, in this case three. All three are the same size, but the bottom one is divided to provide another room and greater interest. The door cut in the bottom box may be plugged with the piece that was cut from the opening, then covered with a floor.

This arrangement of four boxes permits an entrance hall with a patio or terrace above it that is entered from the third-storey room.

That's not really as much as it sounds, for on a day when you're working in the rooms you can take them down from their shelves or cabinets where you keep them, make the arrangement on the dining-room table, and have fun with designing and arranging the rooms, then put them all back out of the way in just minutes after you've finished.

Over years of working with miniature rooms, this has proven my favorite arrangement. If you love to collect and set up the miniature gardens, then some of the others will probably appeal more to you, but I feel that this one gives you everything. On the patio of the second floor many vines and shrubs and trees can be planted, so that you have an oasis of green for the doll family. However, be sure to have doors cut so that the family can pass from one room to another. Windows in the back of the boxes must also be planned ahead if your furniture is going to show off to best advantage; the entire project is something that needs attentive forethought.

Gardening for miniature rooms and dollhouses can become a career in itself if you have the necessary materials. See the listing for Architectural Model Supplies, Inc., in the Appendix.

An example of what is available for the collector who doesn't wish to take the time to make his or her own house is the collection of town-house modular kits pictured on page 29 and marketed by Doreen Sinnett Designs. The basic room kit contains all the material necessary to build a room 15″ × 11″ × 10″ high, comes with a choice of Front A or B, and

A set of templates in various sizes is a boon for the artist who is designing his own layout of rooms. (*Courtesy of Dick Blick Art Supplies*)

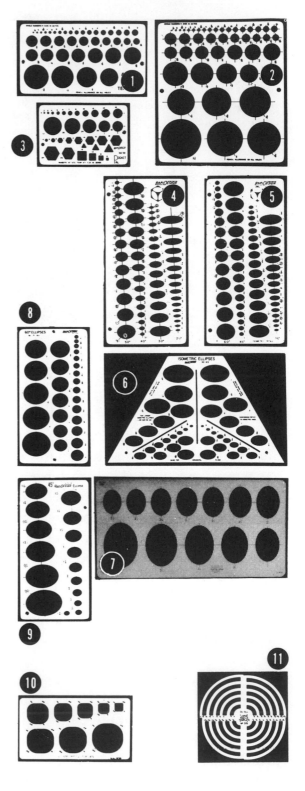

"Module" box rooms such as these marketed by Doreen Sinnett Designs are ideal for the collector who wishes to start with one room and add as his collection grows. (*Photograph courtesy of Doreen Sinnett Designs*)

This basic room by Doreen Sinnett Designs is about 15″ × 11″ × 10″ and comes with a choice of fronts. The kit includes all materials plus magnets for the removable front. (*Photograph courtesy of Doreen Sinnett Designs*)

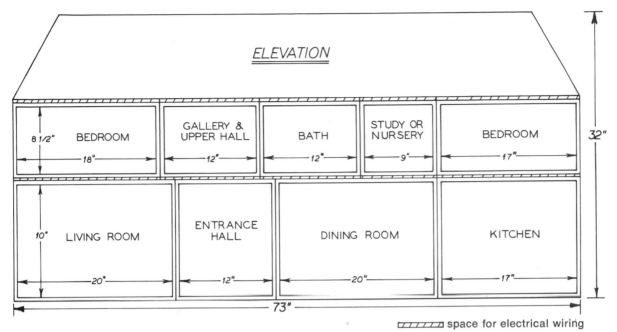

Figure 3
Arrangement of Rooms to Simulate Dollhouse

includes magnets for the removable front. Roof A includes all materials to make the roof, such as "shingles," as shown above, as well as all window parts, as does Roof B. One side of the latter roof comes off for easy access to the attic. The window kits include all materials to finish one window inside and outside.

By going this route, as I mentioned before, the builder has all the fun of building with the basic work done for him. Being able to add one room at a time is another great advantage. Because the designs are so well conceived, the rooms are charming. The dollhouse that will be the result of combining several rooms is, to me, a source of great pride.

3 Miniature Rooms and Vignettes

I should like to correct a misuse of the term *miniature room*, which has come to be used most widely. Many, many students in craft classes who are building small, shallow shadow boxes are calling them miniature rooms when, as a matter of fact, they are not rooms at all, but only *vignettes*, a term which my dictionary defines as "a small, pleasing picture or view."

Susan Rogers Braun, in her excellent book titled *Miniature Vignettes*, recognizes this difference and points it out in the very beginning. In addition, she shows, in color, a number of beautiful vignettes that have been built with miniatures and are exhibited in frames.

Other authors, however, are not so careful. Carol Wenk, a nationally known teacher of craft classes, duplicates her class lectures in a book titled *Shadow-Box Miniature Rooms*, although she isn't creating miniature rooms; she is creating vignettes. They are fine vignettes, very well done, but they are, nevertheless, not rooms since they spotlight only one particular corner or wall of the box.

My only objection to vignettes is that since they portray a limited space, there is little that can be done with them except to look at them once they are finished. Miniature rooms, on the other hand, may be changed and added to or subtracted from as the mood stirs us. An idea may be expanded or contracted and the effect changed completely, since we have a whole room to work with.

This was my reason for selecting boxes of 20″ frontage and 10″ or 11″ depth. I was largely influenced by the miniature rooms in the Bethnal Green Museum in London, England. Most of the single rooms are of a similar size: a Nuremberg kitchen is 2′ 1¾″; a drawing room is 2′ 4″; one butcher's shop (a great favorite in Victorian days) is 2′ 4½″; another butcher's shop, 1′ 9½″. With these dimensions, one can really produce rooms; it seems to me that anything less is merely a vignette.

This distinction is brought out very clearly in several pieces by James Weilepp of Decatur, Illinois. Weilepp, who is a master at the art of miniaturing, does no commercial work, pursuing his hobby, as does Tom Devereaux, merely for his own enjoyment. The first two shadow boxes shown here are similar to the lanthorn houses made by Wes Faurot of Willoughby's 18th Century. These are beautiful spot or vignette pictures encased in lovely frames.

The artist might give a little thought here to touches that indicate the presence of a person in a room, such as the tiny pair of slippers that Willoughby used in one of the lanthorn houses. An open book on a chair also gives the feeling of human habitation. A tea set with cups and saucers provides the same feeling, although the tankard shown in Jim Weilepp's vignette doesn't quite do this.

In the two vignettes made by Carlson's Miniatures of Chicago, this personal feeling is even more evident. Notice the books on the shelves and the sun coming in the window of the little antique shop, and the various accessories in the old general store. See color plates.

Weilepp, in his truly lovely bedroom, has also conveyed a feeling of habitation; note the book on the chair, the coffee pot on the table. Both the bedroom and vignette give the impression of people being not very far away, a requirement of a good miniature room.

The photograph shows Weilepp's ingenious method of providing space that serves for electrical connections and at the same time simulates another room beyond the box. The outside box, which is made of ⅛″ plywood paneling, was built first, complete with a bottom and a roof. Then, the room was constructed; hence, it can be slid in and out of the box. The outer box is 24″ × 14″, and the room is 18″ × 13″, with 3″ on the sides for the hallway and electrical connections. These connections hook up to the fireplace, which actually glows.

The illusion of a real room is even stronger in the second photograph, where sunlight is coming through the window. Here, Weilepp brought a 6″ projection into the room, with the upper part of the wall slanted as for a dormered roof. He has a planted garden in this space at the back of the box. The view through the window is delightful.

The bed will provide many ideas, also. The spread is made from dotted Swiss with rather large tufts and looks exactly right. The heavy lace edging on the canopy is a fine approximation of early hand-crocheted laces.

Two rooms built by Narcissa Thorne as a gift for a collector in the Midwest are actually vignettes. Both foyers are opulently furnished, and the above one has walls of marble. (*Photographs by Elinor Coyle*)

Truly a vignette, this lovely room by Jim Weilepp is made from plywood paneling with a molded border at the bottom. The top is made of plain lumber combined with molding. All of the furniture as well as the beautiful petit-point rug was made by Weilepp.

Another vignette by Jim Weilepp features a firescreen with a handmade petit-point inset. The tiles on the fireplace were made from a clay resembling Sculpy, then painted. Electrical work is hidden at top under the lid.

This shop made by Carlson's Miniatures demonstrates the possibilities of a front wall. The door and all woodwork are beautifully constructed and finished. (*Photograph by Philip Weibler, courtesy of Carlson's Miniatures*)

A general store by Carlson's Miniatures stops just short of being a vignette. Notice the nook jutting into the room at the back; the scene is set around it, and the lighting is hooked up there. The shelves, showcase, and bakery case were made by the Carlsons. (*Photograph by Philip Weibler, courtesy of Carlson's Miniatures*)

Jim Weilepp's lovely country bedroom is a true miniature room. Notice the little shell collection on the far wall, which was made by Mrs. Weilepp. She also made the paintings.

Here the shell containing the room is shown pulled from the outside shell, which has a polished walnut front to hide the space between the room and the box. This space, only 3″, makes it possible to glimpse into another room—in this case, a hallway showing books on a table.

Jim Weilepp's old-time barroom includes every detail found in the originals, including the stairs to the upstairs rooms! Everything, including the eight chairs, was made by Mr. Weilepp.

This full view of the shell containing the bar shows the use of a 6″ space at one end to show the entrance and the scene of the street.

The Fourth Dimension

There is another consideration that must be made in deciding between miniature rooms and vignettes: that of the fourth dimension. Vignettes, because of their extremely shallow composition, must necessarily be thought of as three-sided scenes, and sometimes even less than that since the side walls are usually merely lead-ins.

In the miniature room, however, with a depth ranging from 8″ on up, we have full side walls to provide for, and we often find that the fourth dimension, the front border, also calls for a certain amount of decoration. Thus, we have in Tom Devereaux's Federal bedroom, chairs *with their backs to us*, creating the illusion that we are actually looking in past the fourth wall. The Carlson general store (page 39)

Sitting room by Mary Jane Graham for It's a Small World falls midway between a vignette and a miniature room. The cupboard was covered with illuminated paper, and the chest was made by Mrs. Graham in decoupage with gold and metal trim. The chairs (center) are by Betsy Zorn, and the side chair is by Betty Valentine. Mrs. Graham made the petit-point rug. (*Photograph by Jessie Walker Associates*)

Detail of Mary Jane Graham's library with fabric walls. Notice that the fabric is repeated in the blinds. This box is 24″ × 10″ × 11″. (*Photograph by Jessie Walker Associates*)

The interesting interplay of light and shadow on this gazebo by Mary Jane Graham suggests the many possibilities for such design—potting sheds, porches, arbors. (*Photograph by Jessie Walker Associates*)

This impressive bookstore, inspired by a bookstore print by Anton Pieck, was made by Cynthia Goeltz. Notice how the bookshelves facing to the front bring interest to a fourth dimension. (*Photograph by George Peterson, courtesy of the Beehive Studio*)

creates a similar effect with the showcases pulled flush against the fourth wall, emphasizing the depth of the box.

In the wicker bedroom (page 18), a fourth dimension was created by aligning the chaise longue and the table and chair against the front of the box. In the game room (page 195), a fourth dimension was effected by placing the bridge set against the front of the box.

In the Federal music room (page 62), notice that the sofa, hunt table, and floor globe are placed flush against the front of the box, thus using the fourth dimension fully. This extra dimension adds a great deal to the general interest of the room.

This idea is one well worth considering. I have never found one of the Thorne rooms that used this device, but if Mrs. Thorne had thought of it, I believe she could have used it to good advantage.

4 Choosing a Scale

The scale to be used in your miniature rooms can be either a great comfort, because it provides you with a definite guide for dimensions, or it can be most perplexing, since I can not set up any rules or guidelines. About the only definite thing I can advise is that once you choose the scale you prefer, you should stick to it religiously. The collector who accumulates pieces of different scale is going to end up with a mishmash that will ruin the effect of his miniature rooms.

Mrs. Thorne probably established the 1″-to-1′ scale when she created her beautiful rooms. Her rooms are so perfect, so successful in creating an illusion, that $\frac{1}{12}$ scale seems to be safest for all of us.

However, at almost any miniature show, one will encounter diminutive box rooms made at $\frac{1}{144}$ scale—and furnished in that scale as well. In my first book, *The Collector's Guide to Dollhouses and Dollhouse Miniatures*, I called attention to the work of David W. Dugger of Edmonds, Washington, whose box rooms are considered among the smallest in the world. They are made on a scale of 1″ to 7′. One of them made in this scale measures only 4½″ in width. However, it features a marble floor, a railing with thirty-five hand-carved balusters, a grandfather clock with time-telling hands and weights in the pendulum, and a minuscule chandelier that raises and lowers! The artists do not seem to be able to offer a reason for working in such a small scale, other than that they love to do it.

Bobbie Pieroni's Half-Inch Wild West

Many collectors work in the ½″ scale either because they love the smaller rooms or are cramped for space, but I have never met anyone to equal Bobbie Pieroni of Fresno, California, who has for the past five

A miniature room, "Entry to Elegance," and three vignettes by David W. Dugger, shown here full size, are said to be the smallest in the world. (*Photographs by D. Ross*)

years been building a late-nineteenth-century western town. She wrote me when *The Collector's Guide to Dollhouses and Dollhouse Miniatures* was published that she had started using the ½″ scale because she didn't know what scale to use. She was upset at that time because this scale wasn't mentioned in *The Collector's Guide*. She added that it was only through *The Collector's Guide* that she discovered that she was a builder of box rooms; she knew what she did but not what to call it!

This unbelievable artist works on her western town every day and all day, to use her own words. It has now grown to twenty-seven buildings (miniature rooms) all lighted electrically. Everything was made by Mrs. Pieroni, or as she proudly puts it, everything from fly swatters to brass beds to cakes and pies. "I try very hard not to leave anything out of a building that should be there," she writes. "I have dust balls, spider webs with flies in them, and pencils and socks under a little boy's bed. Detail is very important to me."

The bakery shop shown here, for example, is 8″ wide, 5½″ high, and 9½″ long; the furniture store is 14¼″ long, 11¼″ wide, and 8½″ high. Also, everything a cowboy and his wife could possibly want to buy there Mrs. Pieroni made. The butcher shop is 8½″ long, 7½″ wide, and 5″ high and is well stocked with carcasses that rival those found in old Victorian box rooms. Every imaginable sort of sausage is on the counter, and the scale actually registers weight. The blacksmith shop is 15″ long, 10″ wide, and 6″ high. Every tool a blacksmith would need is there; one can pound on the anvil and build a fire in the forge. Mrs. Pieroni has even included a brothel, only 6″ long and 21″ wide, the reason for these strange dimensions being readily apparent after one thinks about it for a while.

To show us how she worked, she explained that she made lists from old photos and Sears, Roebuck catalogues of the period. Here is her list for the blacksmith shop:

Dirty windows	Hacksaw
Exposed studs	Metal wedge
Beam ceiling, post inside	Screw plates, taps
Sliding door on back wall	Mandrel
Floor uneven	Spoke tenon
Wooden coal bin	Tall rods in barrel
Four worktables	Oil troughs
Light brick forge	Punch
Two anvils	Knife
Horseshoes, new and used	Wagon jack
Barrel of water	Wrenches
Bellows	Screwdrivers

Bucket of water
Bucket of coal
Vises
Grinder bench
Measuring wheel in toolbox
Big grinder
Anvil tools
Drill
Hammers
Tire bender
Drill case
Metal files
Oil cans
Measuring tape

Blowtorch
Machinist tools—calipers, bevel,
    square, emery stone
Pliers
Tin snips
Nippers
Pinchers
Shaping table—knives, shears, chisels,
    meat cleaver, hoe, shovel
Brazier
Tire upsetter
Extra-tall handles
Large lawn clippers

Under the heading "Junk lying around," she lists tools, branding iron, broken pumps, chains, pulleys, gears, coal and shovel, boxes of scrap, metal curls on floor, tin sheets, rope, stove pipe, wire rolls, screen rolls, bells, tool chest, broken tools, lead pouring tools, metal wagon wheel, stack of bricks, rod roller, wagon springs, ball and chain, stove, grease barrel, box of bolts, and many more.

All of these she makes herself, since they are largely unobtainable in the miniature world. Would that you and I could be so meticulous and so patient!

She admits that she has plans for about thirty-eight more buildings and tents. Unbelievable!

Several dealers, notably Louis and Barbara Kummerow of Dollhouses (see Appendix), offer furniture and accessories in the ½" scale, including such accessories as Tiffany-style lamps, brass bathroom fittings, doorknobs, letter drops, and Tiffany-style windows, but you'll have no trouble at all in making the furniture; any pattern in this book can be reduced by half to achieve the size you're trying for.

Everyone is familiar with the $\frac{1}{12}$ scale, so we will skip a discussion of it and go to the 2"-to-1' scale, which is becoming increasingly popular because it accommodates the 10" to 12" Barbie dolls and all their friends and families. Another firm, The Dollhouse Factory in Sunnyvale, California (see Appendix), offers a great deal of furniture and accessories in this scale, and you will, of course, find a great deal of commercially made furniture in the doll departments of toy and hobby stores.

However, the 2" scale is large enough so that you will have no trouble at all in doubling the measurements and making the furniture from the patterns in this book. It doesn't necessarily follow, however,

The seventeenth-century kitchens of early settlers were crowded. Homemakers brightened them with gay curtains and braided rugs. Pie safe at right rear is by Suzanne Ash of Mini-Things.

that you can double the dimensions of your box room to get the proper effect; for some reason or other, it doesn't work out that way. For example, if you have been making miniature rooms in the 1/12 scale and making ceilings 12″ high, things get a little out of hand if you make a ceiling 24″ high for the 2″ scale. This is what it should be, but for even a 12″ doll it seems awfully high. And if you are by any chance using a 10″ doll, she'll be lost in such a cavernous room. Experiment with a cardboard box or a corrugated carton for a bit until you arrive at measurements that seem exactly proper for the doll who is going to live in the miniature room. It must *look* right, not necessarily be mathematically right. Keep that in mind.

As a starter, you might try for a height of 16½″ in your rooms for Barbie or other dolls of that genre. Using this as a beginning, the 20″ width across the front of the box is still quite acceptable, even though I use this same measurement in my rooms on the 1/12 scale. I just happen to like lots of room to work in! You'll find that with the

16½″ ceiling, a depth of about 15″ is good for the 2″-to-1′ scale; it's too cavernous for the ⅟₁₂ scale, because it is not only too deep to reach into comfortably but causes the rear wall to recede until it's difficult to enjoy it. Two-inch-to-the-foot furniture will arrange nicely in a room 15″ deep, however, and will put everything into perspective.

Another miniature room that demonstrates the ways in which we must bend the laws of scale in order to bring about an effective *visual* presentation is the early settler's kitchen. We all know that kitchens (in fact, all rooms) in the early huts had very low ceilings, both for conserving heat and for ease in building. Many such rooms were only 7′ high. However, in our box rooms we have other requirements. One is to keep the rooms of equal shape in order to stack or otherwise display them. Another is, again, our visual effect. A little box only 7″ high is very difficult to see into, and if one wishes to hang things from the beams, such as dried herbs, hams, and little used paraphernalia the homemaker had to duck around in her first kitchen, then the viewer looking in has the feeling he's looking into a forest. Thus, by keeping all of our rooms 12″ high, we may thumb our noses at historical accuracy, but we will end up with a much more pleasing creation.

5 Building Your Own Box Rooms

There are, of course, innumerable builders who will sell you all of the components for your box rooms, all cut and sanded, some complete with nails and screws, so that all you have to do is to put the pieces together. And you'll have great fun in the doing, too. But for real, deep down satisfaction, there is nothing to compare with cutting the lumber yourself and seeing the box take form before your very eyes.

First of all, let's consider the lumber. Some builders, like Mrs. David Thomas of Oak Ridge, Tennessee, like to use ½″ plywood. To me that seems a bit clumsy. Three-eighth-inch plywood, finished on one side, seems to me to be the best selection after much experimentation. I would have preferred ¼″ plywood because it would make the boxes much lighter and easier to handle, but it doesn't work well; ¼″ is too flimsy to hold the necessary screws and nails, and one will soon find himself involved in a lot of repair work if he decides upon the ¼″ material. Notice, too, that I specify plywood finished on one side. This means that the plywood has one side veneer and the other side with defects such as knots. For the perfectionist, this might not be satisfactory. But bear in mind that you are going to cover the walls on the inside with paint or wallpaper or paneling, so the defects won't show. Or, you can use the knotty side on the outside and have veneer to work on inside, and this will be quite all right if you are going to paint the outside. If you're going to stain it, however, you must have veneer on the outside. The savings in cost of the finished-one-side over finished-two-sides is considerable—enough so that it's worth your consideration. Now, we're ready to cut.

If you have a Dremel Moto-Shop, this is no problem. Or you may have a husband who has a basement workshop and will be kind enough to cut the plywood as you direct. Approached the right way, the lumber man will often cut it for you for free or at a small cost, and in large

Figure 4

ONE-HALF 4' x 8' PLYWOOD SHEET
CUTS MOST ECONOMICALLY AS SHOWN

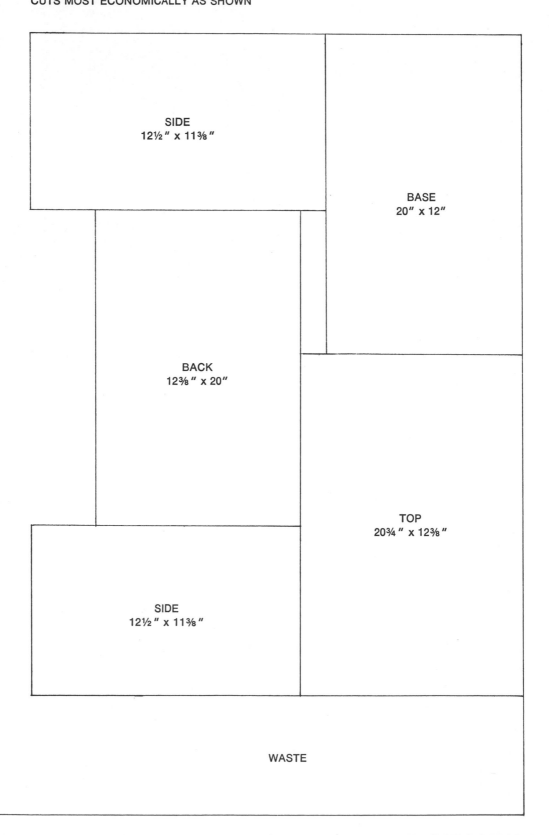

SIDE
12½" x 11⅜"

BASE
20" x 12"

BACK
12⅜" x 20"

TOP
20¾" x 12⅜"

SIDE
12½" x 11⅜"

WASTE

SCALE: 1" = 1'

cities there are discount hardware stores that have tailored-to-measure lumber and do this sort of cutting as a matter of course. Map out your cuts first! See figure 4.

Remember to use your scriber or awl to mark the cut lines; a pencil point, unless very hard, will make a difference in your dimensions. These dimensions are for a 20″ × 12″ box cut from a half sheet of plywood, which will be 4′ × 4′.

Once the base, sides, and back have been cut, we are ready to assemble them.

Place the base on your workbench or work space. Butt the back against it, even at the edges, and glue; then reinforce with ¾″ wire nails. Four nails across the back, evenly spaced, will be about right.

A word of warning here: We have seen many directions for box rooms that direct the builder to use ordinary white craftsman's glue, and such directions can cause you a great deal of trouble. The white craftsman's glue is great for such things as $\frac{1}{12}$-scale furniture that is never going to have to take any strain, and its quick-setting properties are, of course, a godsend. However, a box room must be of a sturdier construction, and we strongly urge you to use a liquid hide glue in the affixing of the various components.

Liquid hide glue is the glue that furniture people use; it makes a joint that is stronger than the wood itself, and since it takes a while to set, you can apply it to the edges of the wood and then hammer in the nails. Allow to dry under a weight or in clamps overnight, and you will have a box that will stand forever. With the back glued and nailed, butt the sides against the base and the back, and glue and nail in the same fashion. Allow the box to set overnight.

At each step here, we'd strongly advise you to use your square and level at every angle and joint, so as to be sure that everything will be "true" when your box is completed. It can be pretty disconcerting to find, when you set the lid, that the corners won't fit, or when you hang your wallpaper, that there's no way to make the stripes hang straight!

When the box is completely dry, there are several methods of preparing for the lid and glass. One way is to cut three ¼″-wide strips; one will be the length of the inside front of the base, and the others will be as long as the inside height of the sides. Glue these so that their far edges are ¾″ in from the front edges of the box. Cut another set and glue these so that they are flush to the edge of the box. This will give you a ¼″ groove in which the glass may be set. The top, or lid, is merely affixed to the back with small hinges so that it may be raised and the ⅛″

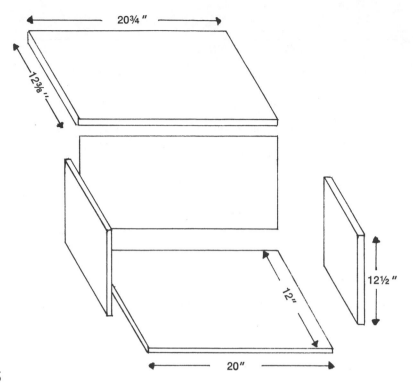

Figure 5

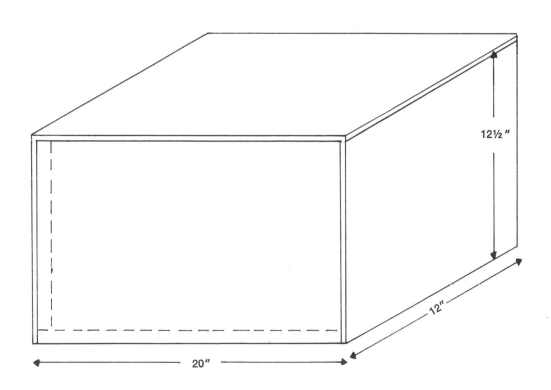

Figure 6

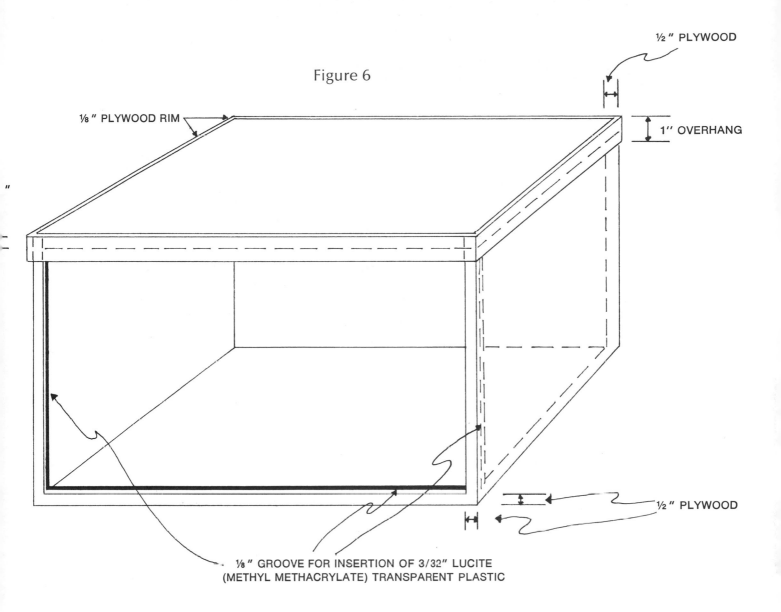

½" PLYWOOD

⅛" PLYWOOD RIM

1" OVERHANG

⅛" GROOVE FOR INSERTION OF 3/32" LUCITE
(METHYL METHACRYLATE) TRANSPARENT PLASTIC

½" PLYWOOD

BOX ROOM BY MRS. DAVID THOMAS OF ½" PLYWOOD
SHOWING "LID TYPE" CONSTRUCTION

glass removed when you wish to work on the room inside. Mrs. Thomas
prefers to affix a ⅛" plywood rim to the lid, or top, so that the lid is
actually a shallow box that fits over the top of the room and is easily
removed. Mrs. Thomas also prefers to use her router to open a ⅛"
groove for insertion of the glass.

Ron Muckerman perfected another idea that I have come to prefer
for the closing of my rooms. After a box that is to be opened from the
top is finished, he cuts a ¾"-wide strip from ¾" wood and fits it to the
top and bottom with mitered corners. The strips for the two sides are
cut ⅜" longer than the box edges to which they are to be glued. The

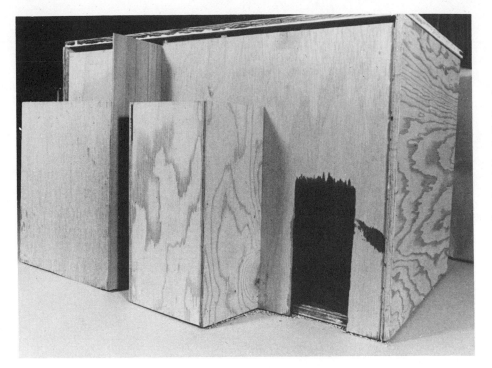

The back of the box containing the early settler's kitchen illustrates a way of adding depth to the boxes; this was Mrs. Thorne's favorite method of providing backlighting. The small box at center holds the fireplace that juts out from the box. The bay at left houses the breakneck staircase. The outside of the box has not yet been finished.

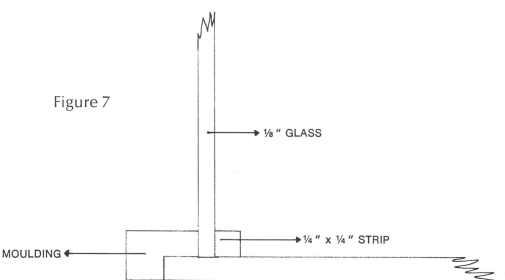

Figure 7

⅛ " GLASS

¼ " x ¼ " STRIP

MOULDING

ends of these strips, too, are mitered. The two sides and the bottom are then glued to the edges of the box, mitered corners meeting, the sides being ⅜" longer at the top than the sides of the box.

On the strip that will be glued to the top, or front edge of the box top, Muckerman routs out a ⅜" indentation (⅜" deep, ⅜" from the edge of the strip) the length of the strip. You will notice that this cuts into the mitered ends of the strip. Glue to the front edge of the top, top edges flush. You will find that this fits down over the mitered ends of the side pieces, forming a perfect frame, if your miters have been correct.

The ¼″ strips are then installed ¼″ in from the outside edges of the box as described above to form a groove to hold the glass.

Framing the Room

You will notice that this gives you a perfect frame around your room. It may be left natural, or the outside and inside edges may be painted or gilded. If you wish to further carry a bit of color or finish into the room, the little ¼″ strips which form the backstop of the glass slide may also be painted.

I have, however, in many instances used this as a base for constructing a more ornamental frame. In the Japanese room, for example, I stained the entire box, including the front frame, and then glued a gold decoupage border over the front. It has a delicate, fragile look that seems to complement the Japanese decor.

Catalogues from either Craftsman Wood Service or Constantine's (see Appendix) will illustrate many types of picture-frame moldings that will fit over this base frame perfectly; one has only to cut the strips to fit, miter the corners, and glue. When using the frame molding in this manner, however, it is well to make certain that its outside edges are not too wide, for in doing this you are extending the edge of your box again. It does, however, make a beautiful finish, much like the heavy gilt Victorian frames that were used in some of the Thorne rooms.

Some builders actually construct a picture frame to set onto the front of the box. This makes a permanent closing, however, so in using it you must arrange for another opening from which to work. To accomplish this, the builder uses any preferred picture-frame molding and constructs the frame to fit the front of the box room. The frame is then painted or finished in any preferred way, and glass is set in it as glass would be for a picture, except that we use the little so-called glazier's points to fasten the glass in the frame. The frame may then be affixed permanently to the front of the box, or attached on hinges if you wish to open the box at the front.

This brings us to another consideration for the opening of the box. I like to work from the top, and consequently I have the top of the box hinged. Many builders of box rooms prefer to have the back hinged, and I know one builder who has both the back and the front hinged. A front that opens provides for easy placement of the furniture. If a back is open, the back wall may be indented an inch or so, and the electrical components can then be fastened to the back wall. Then the second, or outside, wall is hinged to provide access to this space. This arrangement works beautifully, but make certain that the front and back do not open on the same side; this could overbalance the box and perhaps trigger a spill.

PART II

6 Federal Music Room, ca.1789

At the end of the eighteenth century there were a great number of cabinetmakers and carvers who had come to this country from England and Germany. Grinling Gibbons with his masterpiece wood decorations was a little earlier, but much fine work was being done in the great houses of both North and South.

Thus, when you set yourself the task of reproducing a room from a house of this period, you are giving yourself a chance to exhibit your skill and, in the case of a room such as our music room, your good taste as well.

A music room was found in almost all of the great houses of the period, because music was one of the arts that was in great vogue. In fact, the collections of musical instruments from the Continent were a cause of rivalry among the top hostesses of the day.

In the Federal music room, there is a harp made by the late Joseph Gray. On the table in the foreground the guitar and banjo are both made of Toledo ware from Spain. The brass horn on the footstool in the background came from Germany. These are metal instruments that it would be impossible for you to make; you will just have to keep an eye open as you make the rounds of the sales and pick up what you can. The violin on the piano stool was made by Mr. Charles Graves ("Jini") and this, too, I suggest you buy; in my experience, a dozen efforts have failed to provide an acceptable instrument.

Harold's Handcrafted Instruments (see Appendix) offers a complete list of instruments of fine quality, from a cello with bow to a zither. There is a stereopticon with a real stereo view, and their harp is particularly fine.

As for the room itself, however, we can "go to town" with our talents. Let's start, as usual, with the floor. Floors in this period were

There is great pleasure in producing such elegance as this music room of 1789. The Palladian window is simply installed over a wall mural by Chestnut Hill. The arches are of plaster, marketed by Grandmother Stover.

generally highly polished and left plain, with Oriental rugs or floor cloths laid over them. We used ½" pine planks without beveling the edges (see photograph) in ¹⁄₁₆"- or ³⁄₃₂"-thick wood and laid them, beginning at the front of the box and using Constantine's veneering glue. As I mentioned before, great care must be exercised to be sure the glue is spread very thinly and evenly if you wish to lay the floor before finishing (my own preference) so that no glue comes up between the planks; the wood will not take a stain if glue has touched it.

Let dry under weights to prevent warping. When the glue is entirely dry (preferably overnight), apply one coat of varnish stain; golden oak gives a nice not-too-dark effect. When this is dry, sand lightly with No. 400 sandpaper, dust carefully, then apply another coat. This can go on for as long as your patience holds; some miniaturists use eight coats on floors, but I feel that four is sufficient; eight gives a finish good enough for furniture. When the last coat has dried and been carefully dusted, spray with a light coat of Sani-Wax Lemon Oil Finish. Let stand a few minutes, then rub down with a piece of felt from an old felt hat. (One of your husband's old hats will provide material for several jobs, and he'll never miss it.)

Both arch and fireplace are made of plaster. These faithful reproductions are by Grandmother Stover.

Chestnut Hill's music room of the same period is equally impressive but is made in a shallower box, only 8″ deep. Hence, it can be hung on the wall.

A somewhat inconsequential but nevertheless most interesting question arises in this matter of laying floors: should we place the boards crosswise, from left to right, or lengthwise, from front to back?

It would seem to be entirely a matter of personal preference, and my preference has always been to lay the boards crosswise since this will visually widen the box. This also agrees with the professional's preference for laying the boards the long way of the room.

However, many miniaturists, including the expert Jim Weilepp of Decatur, Illinois, lay the floors from front to back, which, of course, carries the eye to the back of the box and so increases the illusion of depth.

I wanted to use the plaster arches from the Grandmother Stover line for this room because they add such a professional touch, so these were carefully measured against the end walls of the room and the proper opening cut with a small jeweler's keyhole saw.

This was a period when many people were ordering hand-painted wallpaper from Europe. You can make your own from the several designs offered by Joe Hermes and others, or use, as I did, Chestnut Hill's (see Appendix for these suppliers) beautiful hand-painted lengths; one will be ample, with a bit left over, for a 20″ × 10″ room. Measure 2¼″ from the floor up on the walls all around the room and paint to harmonize with your furniture and paper. You may prefer to use acrylic paint because you can mix your own shade; acrylic, too, gives a slightly rougher, most attractive finish. I used a shade called Mount Vernon green from Phelan Paint Company. But be careful to protect the floor when you are applying paint.

Now apply the paper from the ceiling to the edge of the paint. Place the arches and glue, using large (3″) Esterbrook or Boston Ball clips to hold the arches in place until set. Apply a chair rail painted white enamel to cover the joining of paper and paint, being careful to make the chair rail exactly meet the arches. When the arches are applied in this fashion, please notice, the paper has not been cut from the openings. When the arches are dry, carefully cut around them and the opening, to remove the paper. Always use a very sharp X-acto knife and always cut from inside to outside or you'll have a rough edge. This way you'll have a perfect opening.

The arches may be painted before installing, but I didn't think this necessary; they have a very fine finish, retail for about eight dollars per pair. Apply the white enameled baseboard to exactly meet the arches.

Cut to measure, enamel, and apply the ceiling cornice.

Paint the inside of the top of the box and apply one of the medallions available from Craftsman Wood Service or Constantine's. Paint the whole ceiling with one more coat. Screw in one of the smallest available screw eyes (probably ¼″) in the center of the medallion and hang the lighting fixture from this. If you are making an electrical connection, this should be brought down from the outside of the top of the box to connect with the chandelier.

Palladian Window

I really wouldn't advise you to try to make your own Palladian window, even though they are a bit expensive when purchased from one who makes them professionally. The one shown is from Howard Pierce of The Workshop (see Appendix) and is the only one offered anywhere as far as I know. It makes a beautiful addition to any room or house and comes complete with acrylic resin film and attached molding. It is, however, made to be applied flat to the wall, and I used it so in this room, but you will notice in the photo that this gives a very shallow effect. I believe that it would be worthwhile to trace the outline of the window on the wall after papering and cut out with a keyhole saw ⅛″ inside the outline. This would give you the ⅛″ for installing the window, and a shallow box about an inch deep and papered all around could be mounted behind it. The effect, I think, would be somewhat more realistic.

Opinions vary as to the curtaining of a Palladian-style window. In some old houses, draperies were hung only over the two side panels. In some, a gathered curtain was installed over the semicircular window at top. I have seen one where this was done, and very full curtains were hung from the top of the window straight across and then looped back.

My own personal feeling is that the window is so beautiful that curtains are not only unnecessary but an overadornment, even more so if the scene behind the window is especially attractive.

Spinet Piano

Materials Needed for This Project

1 piece ¾″ wood, 6″ × 3″
1 piece ⅛″ wood, 6″ × 6″

This basic spinet piano is an easy piece for the beginner to turn out. It may be elaborated by the addition of inlay or carving. The design is classic, fitting almost any age.

1 length ¼″ × ¼″ wood, 1′ long
1 piece ½″ wood, 4⅝″ × ⅝″
1 length ¹⁄₁₆″ brass rod, 1′ long
1 small piece (about 1″) brass rod or 3 brass or gold oat beads
4 brass 2-mm oat beads
1 small strip black construction paper
X-acto knife
Glue and rubber cement
No. 400 sandpaper
Stain, lacquer, or varnish

Cut all wood pieces; then sand, stain, and finish to a "piano" finish. Then shape the legs and stain and finish.

Purely for decoration, rout or chisel out a border along *A* at the bottom along the dotted line. One-eighth-inch inlaid borders are a nice decoration in this spot.

Glue *D* atop *A*, exactly centered and flush with the back. Glue *B* against *D*, exactly centered, flush with back. Glue *C1* against *B*. Make sure that everything is exactly centered.

Figure 8
Spinet Piano

LATE 18th CENTURY

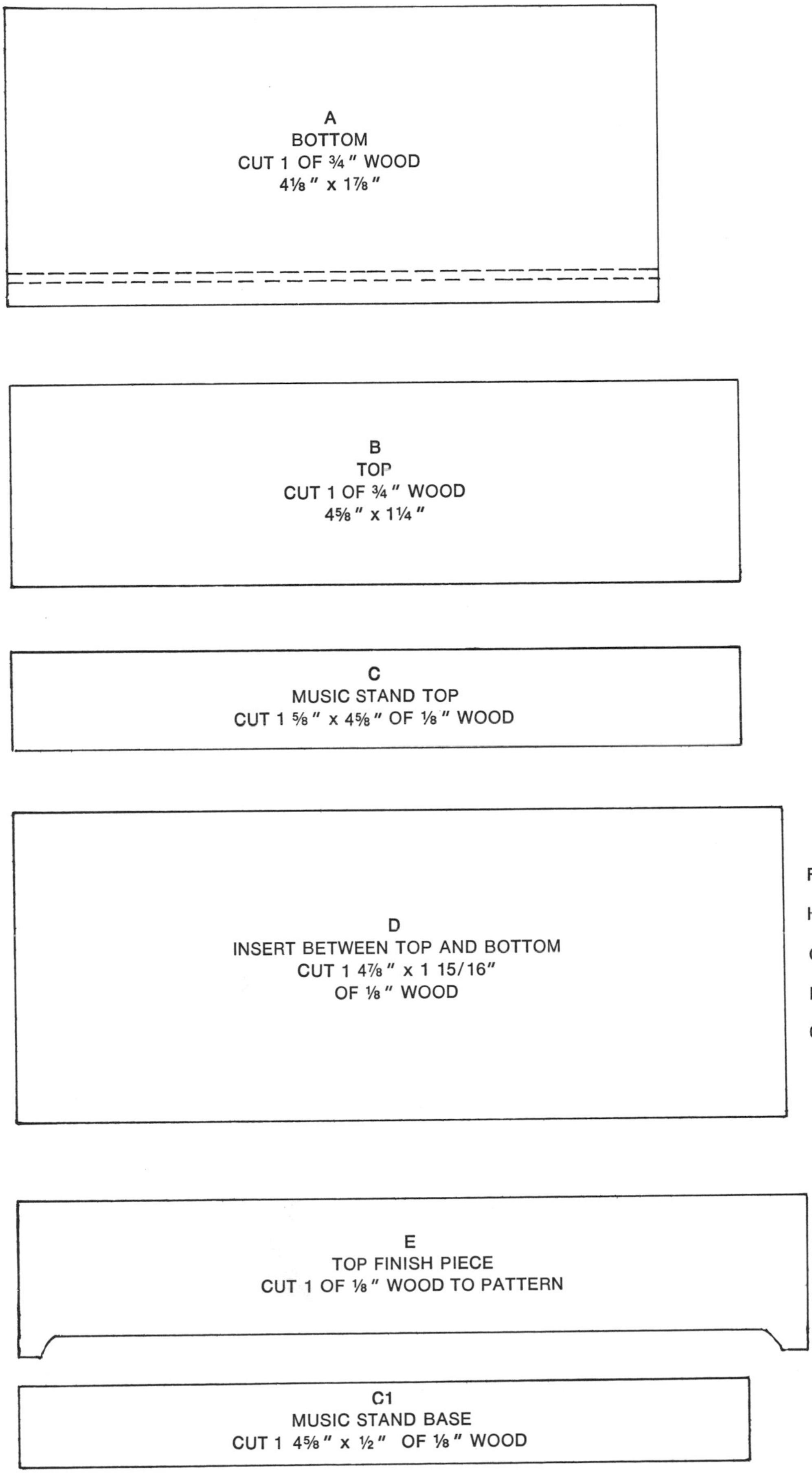

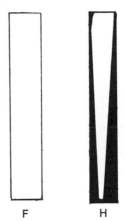

F   H

A
BOTTOM
CUT 1 OF ¾ " WOOD
4⅛ " x 1⅞ "

B
TOP
CUT 1 OF ¾ " WOOD
4⅝ " x 1¼ "

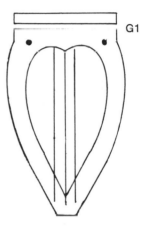

G1

C
MUSIC STAND TOP
CUT 1 ⅝ " x 4⅝ " OF ⅛ " WOOD

BRACE

G

D
INSERT BETWEEN TOP AND BOTTOM
CUT 1 4⅞ " x 1 15/16"
OF ⅛ " WOOD

F: LEG TOP BAR, CUT 2 OF ⅛ " WOOD

H: LEG, CUT 4 OF ¼ " WOOD

G: PEDAL LYRE, CUT 1 OF ⅛ " WOOD

BRACE AT BOTTOM,

CUT 1 ½ " x ⅜ " OF ⅛ " WOOD

E
TOP FINISH PIECE
CUT 1 OF ⅛ " WOOD TO PATTERN

C1
MUSIC STAND BASE
CUT 1 4⅝ " x ½ " OF ⅛ " WOOD

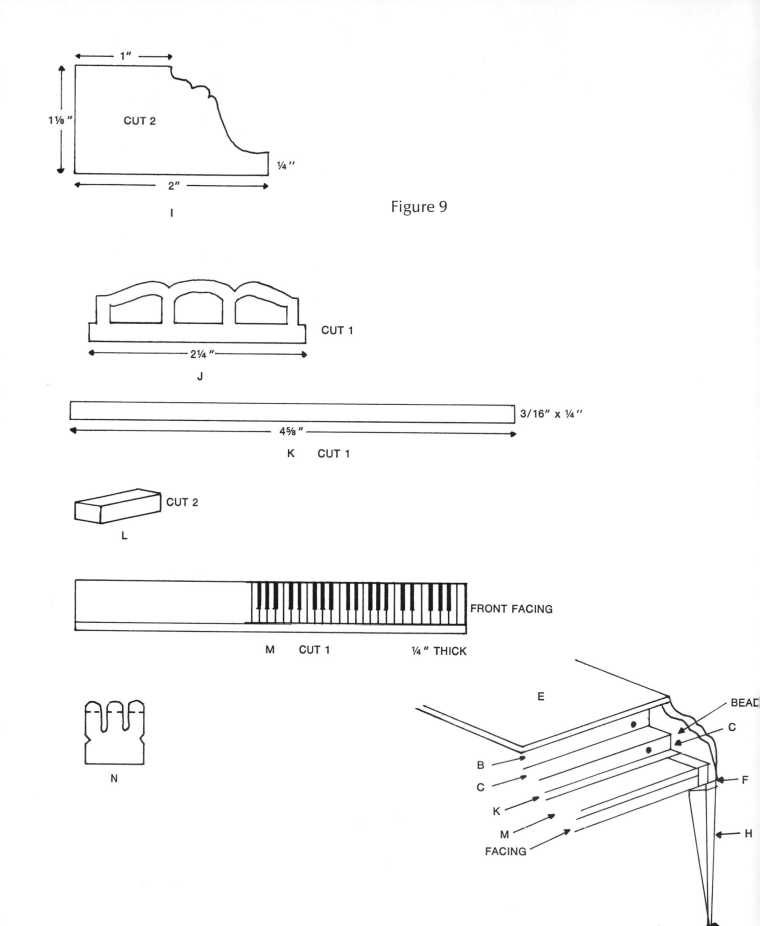

1"

1⅛"

CUT 2

¼"

2"

I

Figure 9

CUT 1

2¼"

J

3/16" x ¼"

4⅝"

K   CUT 1

CUT 2

L

FRONT FACING

M   CUT 1   ¼" THICK

N

E

BEAD

B

C

C

K

F

M

H

FACING

Glue *I* pieces at each end of the top, flush with the back. These should exactly meet the edges of *D*.

Glue *E* against the top of *B*, exactly centered. There should be a tiny overlap at front and sides. The back should be flush.

Glue *C* against *C1*. These should fit exactly in length, but *C1* should overlap just a bit in front.

Glue shaped legs to each end of *F* and then attach to the underside of *D* at the space open there. *F* should reach from back to front.

Glue the lyre back to the brace, centered. Cut three pieces of $\frac{1}{16}$″ brass rod to overlap the length of the lyre and glue to the back of the lyre so that from the front they seem to be fixed into the lyre. Glue the lyre back against *G1* (cut from $\frac{1}{8}$″ wood to fit the top of the lyre) and then against the underside of the piano, into the joint between *A* and *D*.

Cut *N* from heavy brass foil and glue or tack against the bottom of the lyre (or use 2- or 3-mm oat beads, gold color, glued against the brace).

Now for the keyboard: Glue *K* onto the top of *D*, which protrudes from the music-stand base, up against the music-stand base. Glue the two small squares (*L*) into the ends against the side pieces and *K*.

Cut a piece of $\frac{1}{4}$″ wood $\frac{1}{2}$″ wide (*M*). Miniaturist Joen Ellen Kanze (see Appendix) offers a printed keyboard for fifty cents that may be glued directly to the wood, and I would strongly advise using this. However, if you prefer to do your own, paint the top and front of the keyboard piece a pearly white. Starting from the center, using an X-acto knife, score keys $\frac{1}{16}$″ apart to the right, then $\frac{1}{16}$″ apart to the left. Make the scores about $\frac{1}{16}$″ deep. Using heavy black construction paper, cut a strip $\frac{5}{16}$″ wide, then slice into $\frac{1}{16}$″ pieces. Glue these to the keyboard, using tweezers, with rubber cement as shown, starting at right. The pattern is three, two, three, two, and so on.

Many miniaturists, Mel Prescott prominent among them, have found sources for very fine toothed combs in black and white and use the teeth for the keyboard. I prefer the above, however, since it is not nearly so bulky.

In a miniature of this many pieces, it is especially important that every single measurement be exact to a hair's breadth; otherwise, you will find some places where pieces don't fit. When the pieces are all cut and stained, it might be well to fit them together before gluing to make certain that the fit is perfect.

Notice in the photo, also, that we have rounded off the edges of some pieces, i.e., the front edges of *I*, the front edges of *C* and *E*, and the front edges of *L*.

The ornate square piano shown here is made by Mel Prescott. It shows beautiful inlay and wood finish. (*Photograph by Elinor Coyle*)

If you prefer, you might cut one more piece of ⅛″ wood the exact distance between the two *L* pieces, sand and finish, and glue this to the front of the keyboard. Makes a nice finish.

The finishing touch is the little music stand applied to the top of *C*. Notice that on the "square" piano by Mel Prescott shown in our photo a brass medallion about 2″ long has been mounted as a music stand; this is appropriate for such an ornate instrument and might even be used on the piano you have made. Simply cut a ⅛″ × ⅛″ piece of wood the length of the music stand, and glue about halfway back on the music-stand top (*C*) after sanding and staining to match the rest of the piano. If you are using a brass-medallion music stand, glue this against the support.

If you are using a wood stand as I did on my piano, however, cut the outside measurement according to the pattern. Trace the pattern of the cutout onto the wood, using 1⁄16″- or ⅛″ wood. Make the cutout portions using a very sharp X-acto knife or by drilling a tiny hole in the center of the cutout and inserting an X-acto keyhole saw blade to cut around the design. This might even be cut from the 1⁄16″ wood using a pair of small nail scissors, but once the cutting is accomplished, you must sand and stain the music stand. I found that the 1⁄16″ wood was exceedingly difficult to handle in the sanding. Edges here are not rounded; they are left sharp. When this last little piece is completed, glue it to the brace that you've mounted on the music-stand top (*C*) and you're finished.

Piano Stool

During this period, piano stools and benches were practically unheard of, dainty chairs being most used with the piano. I have photographed this particular stool, however, since it can be used in rooms of so many other periods. Also, it is fun to make.

Cut a 1½″ circle from ¼″ wood for the top. Drill a ⅛″ hole in the exact center, insert a ⅛″ bolt ¾″ long, and glue securely.

Cut a 1″ circle from ¼″ wood for the undersupport; drill a ⅛″ hole in the exact center, then rout out so it will take a ⅛″ hexagonal bolt. Fit into the wood and glue securely.

Figure 10
Piano Stool

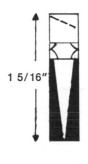

1 5/16″

Legs from the ¼″ dowel are shaped as shown, ¼″ left square at the top, then a turn whittled in 3/16″. Balance of the leg is simply trimmed down to a nice foot, then sanded smooth.

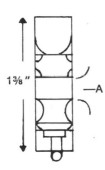

1⅜″

—A

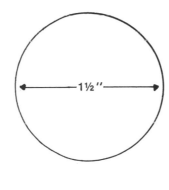

1½″

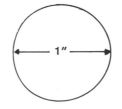

1″

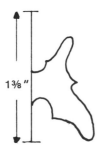

1⅜″

Cut four pieces of ¼" dowel each 1⁵⁄₁₆" long. These are the legs; they may be simply turned as shown in the photo, with the bottom ¼" being rounded off, or cut as shown in the drawing. Also cut four pieces of ⅛" dowel. Sand and finish all pieces.

Slant off the top of each leg so it will fit against the under support at an angle. Glue onto the undersupport, allow to dry, then glue the ¹⁄₁₆" dowels between the legs as supports. Allow to dry.

Pad the top with just a bit of cotton. Cut a circle of satin or velveteen 2" in diameter. Spread glue along the outside edge of the top, then stretch the upholstery circle over the cotton and down around the edge, bringing it down even, so there are no pleats. Fasten with a rubber band until dry, then trim around the edge of the top very closely. Cut a piece of gold or other braid long enough to go around the top, spread the velvet edge with glue, and set the braid in place so as to cover the edge of the upholstery material, with about a ¼" overlap. Fasten with a rubber band until the glue is dry.

The top of the piano stool with the bolt in it will just fit into the bottom with the nut in it, so that the stool may be raised and lowered. It is imperative, however, that the holes for the bolt and nut be exactly centered, or the top won't set straight and turn free.

The second piano stool doesn't turn, but is somewhat prettier. Cut the 1½" circle and cover as directed above. Stain and finish on the bottom. Cut a center spindle from a ¼" square of wood 1⅜" long and whittle out to make a graceful leg as in figure 10. Cut four legs from ⅛" wood as shown. Sand and finish all pieces, then glue the legs to the spindle at *A* so the stool sets firm.

7 Antebellum Parlor

The antebellum parlor shown in the photo was actually copied, piece by piece, from a house in Mechanicsburg, Pennsylvania. The plant stands are made of tin can strips. The curtains and cornices are true to the period. The fire screen at right is a copy of a Victorian museum piece, and the scene is hand painted.

The carpet is a Brussels actually made in Belgium and imported; similar carpets in different tones will be found in many of my boxes. The little cherry-blossom bonsai on the whatnot at the center of the back wall was imported from Japan, and the little Buddhas are from my mini-Buddha collection.

The glass domes covering bird figures on the mantel and the one on the whatnot at right rear are merely plastic prizes from nickel candy machines. However, domes and bell jars now may be obtained in fine hand-blown glass. A base is sometimes found on the dome itself when it's rescued from the candy machine; otherwise, it can easily be made by cutting a circle of similar size from $\frac{1}{8}''$ wood and beveling gently around the edge with your Moto-Shop.

The upholstered sofa and chairs are a one-of-a-kind set and were made for me by Lucille Spinka (see Appendix). The set was copied from Victorian museum pieces, and they are made of walnut and upholstered with deep purple velvet, which was then hand painted.

In the early nineteenth century before formal and practical educations were acceptable for women, their schooling mainly consisted of cultural pursuits, such as embroidery, drawing, and painting, which was particularly popular. "Theorem" painting, so called because it presented a problem, was the most pursued.

Painting on velvet takes just a bit of experience, but once you catch the "feel" of it, many projects are possible: the painted velvet

This antebellum parlor is an exact copy of a room in a house in Mechanicsburg, Pennsylvania. The wall covering of dress satin is a fine foil for the somewhat over-elegant furnishings.

The parlor set is a one-of-a-kind creation by Lucille Spinka. Carving is kept simple so as to bring out the elegance of the painted-on velvet upholstery.

hangings popular in the twenties, the ornamental screens of the thirties, the panels above mirrors, and so on.

To start, you need a piece of velvet, naturally, but the Spinkas upholstered their furniture first and then painted the finished pieces. They did it freehand, but you may want to trace a pattern using yellow or light purple dressmaker's carbon. *Typing carbon will not work*; it will slip and smear on the velvet.

Use good, flat, short-bristled sable oil brushes and fairly thin oil paint. Use almost a dry brush; if there is too much paint on the brush, it will catch in the nap of the velvet and clog in blobs. The soft texture of the velvet must never be lost in the painting.

Whether you have lightly chalked the design onto the velvet or are painting freehand, go over each detail, finishing each color before going on to another. The light places you notice in the photo are silver-painted highlights; other colors include soft greens and a deep rose.

Figure 11
Design for Painting on Velvet

CENTER OF DESIGN
REPEAT FROM HERE

Painting on fabric is a technique that requires a bit of practice, but one which you will especially enjoy once you've mastered it. Practice on pieces of scrap velvet until you feel you're ready to work on the upholstered pieces. Good pieces to practice on are panels at the top of miniature mirrors, or tiny 1″-square pillow covers; either may be discarded until you've acquired some proficiency.

Small stems, scrolls, and leaf veins may be added after the basic painting is completed by using a small, round pointed sable brush and very thin paint—thinned with turpentine. You'll find the effect, especially on pillows, charming.

Corner Whatnot Shelf

This whatnot shelf, copied from a museum piece, was made by Mary Frances Cochran, one of the truly great miniaturists, from black walnut grown on her mother's farm in West Virginia. The little decorated egg on the top shelf was actually made within a quail egg. The flowers under glass are encased in a plastic cover from a candy machine. The little decoys were carved from blocks of balsa wood with an X-acto knife and then painted. The fan on the bottom shelf is made of papier-mâché and is discussed on pages 81–82.

Mrs. Cochran made the two sides of the shelf so that they fit together. They need only shelves to make the piece complete. The wood is then stained, rubbed, and polished, then stained again until you have the finish you desire. At least four coats of stain are necessary; perfectionists will use up to eight.

Cornices

The lace curtains in this room were made from very fine 3″ lace that was originally used on an old wedding dress. Lace makes an especially fine material for curtains, since if you look assiduously, you will find some finished with scallops on both sides. The curtains here are hemmed at top and bottom, then threaded on small brass tubing (or ⅛″ dowels), and hung on the tiniest of shoulder hooks or cup hooks (no more than ¼″) at the top of the windows. A three-sided box is then made of ⅛″ balsa wood, making sure that it is deep enough (on the sides) to go over the hooks. The covering material here is a braid found in the drapery department of a department store. There it was meant to

The Victorian whatnot shelf by Mary Frances Cochran is made of black walnut and was shaped with a jigsaw.

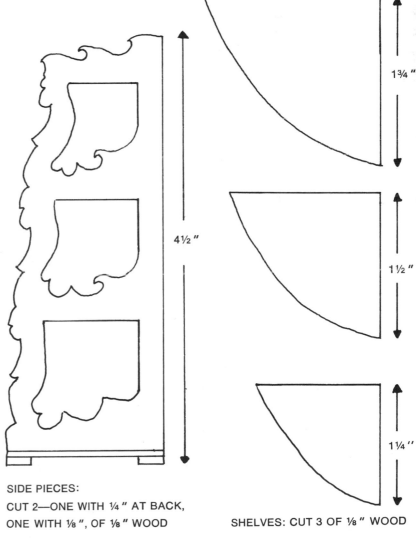

4½"

1¾"

1½"

1¼"

SIDE PIECES:

CUT 2—ONE WITH ¼" AT BACK,
ONE WITH ⅛", OF ⅛" WOOD

SHELVES: CUT 3 OF ⅛" WOOD

Figure 12
Victorian Whatnot Shelf

enhance the edge of the draperies but was exactly the right size (½″ deep) for the cornices. This was glued to the cornices, which were then attached with a quick-drying glue. You may have to hold them in place for five minutes or so until they are stuck in place, but this is the easiest and quickest way I know to finish a window. You can always read a book while you're holding them!

The wall covering in this room is particularly worthy of note. Unable to find a paper that seemed appropriate and being a bit bored with the usual miniature papers of this period, I used a heavy satin that had originally been a cocktail dress. If you use a material such as this, experiment on a scrap to make certain that the glue won't stain through it to the side that shows; then use ordinary wallpaper wheat paste. As I instruct with other rooms, cut the back to fit exactly, allowing ½″ at each end. Glue to the back wall, pressing the overage well into the corners. *Do not use a damp cloth to smooth the material as directed with wallpapers.* Merely press smooth with your brayer; then let dry under weights. Then cut the sides to fit exactly between the front edge and the corners, and apply in the same fashion.

Materials Needed for This Project

1 length ⅛″ hard wood, such as walnut, mahogany, or cherry, 2″ wide and about 9″ long
Stain or varnish
Any good glue that dries clear
Fine steel wool for polishing
Lemon-oil wax
Jigsaw or fine keyhole saw

Cut the two side pieces exactly the same except at the back measurement; here, one piece should be ¼″ wide and the other should be ⅛″ wide.

Trace the design onto the wood; cut a small hole in each of the openings in the design and carefully saw out the design with a small keyhole or jeweler's saw. Sand until smooth. Glue the two pieces together in a butt joint, the piece with the ⅛″ back measurement against the one with the ¼″ back measurement. Take care that no glue oozes onto the wood, or it won't take the stain. Stain and polish. Stain and polish the shelves and glue into the frame.

If you have a router, a nice finish for the edge of the shelves is to rout out a little band along the curved edge. Or just bevel the curved edge with sandpaper or your Moto-Shop.

Your Own Family Album

The design of the family album here, by Charles Claudon, is based on an actual family album from the latter part of the Victorian period, although the number of pages has been greatly reduced.

Materials Needed for This Project

    Cardboard
    Tracing paper
    White typing paper
    India ink
    Fine-tipped pen
    Colored pencils
    Polaroid camera and black-and-white film
8 old photographs
    Velvet or other fabric
    White glue
    Acrylic paints
    Printed paper to use as endpapers
    Deft clear wood finish

With the India ink, trace the page designs (*A*) onto the tracing paper. When finished, turn the design to the wrong side and color it; using the wrong side makes the colors more subtle. Claudon used red and vermillion for the flowers, olive green for the leaves and stems, and ocher for the surrounding areas.

Figure 13
Family Album

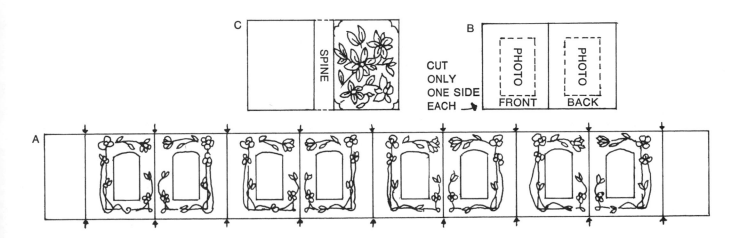

Cut out the page section (*A*) in one long strip, then cut out the openings into which the pictures will go. Carefully accordion-fold the entire strip, making it into four pages with two end pieces.

Select the photos to be included in the album. (One of the noteworthy things about Claudon's album is that he used actual photos of his family in the book.) Arrange them on the floor so that all eight pictures will be included in one photograph if possible. Stand directly over your pictures with your Polaroid, focus, and take your picture. Develop the print according to Polaroid instructions.

When dry, cut out the individual pictures to the size shown in *B*. (Note: *B* shows the front *and* back of *one* backing sheet.) Mount the pictures onto their backings where indicated and then glue the backings between the pages. Set aside to dry.

Cut the front and back covers from the cardboard, as shown in *C*. Next, cut out a piece of typing paper the size of the entire cover section laid out flat. This will serve as a cover backing. Glue the cardboard in place on the backing.

Now cut a piece of velvet (Claudon chose forest green) or other material about ¼″ larger than the cover section. Glue it carefully onto the paper side.

When the cover is dry, cut a small square from the top and bottom of the page-spine section (*C*). This will allow for the material in the spine area and enable the pages and spine to glue firmly to the typing-paper spine. Glue the pages in place. Glue down the front and back flaps to the cardboard. Cut out two endpapers from the printed paper, approximately the same size as the page backing sheets (*B*).

If you used velvet, brush the front cover with one coat of Deft, allow it to get tacky, then smooth the nap down and let dry. Using acrylics, paint a design onto the cover. When dry, begin applying several coats of Deft, allowing each to dry at least thirty minutes. Continue until a smooth surface resembling leather has been achieved—about ten to fifteen coats. Polish with a soft, dry cloth. This is done only on the front cover; in most old albums the back was left in velvet.

In another old family album in the author's collection, the front cover is decorated with a tiny jeweled heart cut from an earring. A catch is fashioned from a tiny ¼″ link from a gold necklace. The link is opened, threaded through a tiny (⅛″) brass eye, then closed again. The opening at the bottom of the eye is cut off and the end sharpened a bit so that it may be forced into the edge of the back cover. A straight brass pin is forced into the front cover and left projecting just a bit. The link from the necklace hooks over the pinhead to form a fastening for the book. If your book is thicker than the ¼", just find a link that is long enough to fit.

Victorian Fan

Betty Spice of Wadsworth, Ohio, entered this graceful Victorian papier-mâché fan in the 1975 Originality Contest staged by the *Dollhouse and Miniature News*. Typical of Victoria's rococo world, it is highly decorated on its glimmering black lacquered surface. You'll want several in your rooms.

Materials Needed for This Project
1 piece lightweight card stock or paper
1 wooden Q-tip, 1¼" long
   Tester's black enamel paint
   Acrylic paints
   Glue
   File or emery board
   Razor saw (or razor blade)

Figure 14
Victorian Fan

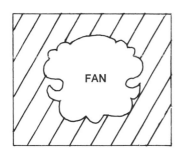

Fan Pattern: Cut one
from card stock or paper.
Cut inside outline.
Paint with black enamel on
both sides.

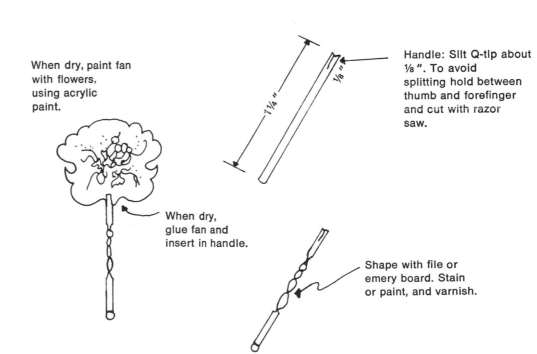

When dry, paint fan
with flowers,
using acrylic
paint.

When dry,
glue fan and
insert in handle.

Handle: Slit Q-tip about
⅛". To avoid
splitting hold between
thumb and forefinger
and cut with razor
saw.

Shape with file or
emery board. Stain
or paint, and varnish.

First, trace the fan pattern and cut from the card stock or paper. Paint the resulting shape with black enamel on both sides. When dry, paint the fan with flowers or an appropriate scene, using the acrylic paint. Paint both sides; dry propped up against a saucer edge.

For the handle, slit the Q-tip about ⅛″ down from the top; to avoid splitting, hold the tip between your thumb and forefinger and cut with the razor saw or razor blade. Shape the tip with the file or emery board, making little rounds on the handle at intervals. Stain or paint; then varnish.

When dry, slip the fan into the slit in the handle and glue. Let dry before using.

8 Art Nouveau Bedroom

I am always a little puzzled why so few miniaturists work in the Art Nouveau period—say, from 1890 to 1910. Mrs. Thorne did many rooms in this period, and I know she loved the sensuous, flowing lines that the period expressed.

In 1861, William Morris had set up the arts and crafts movement, which in itself is sufficient for miniaturists to give the trend some attention. As the arts and crafts societies, the shops, the arts centers, the schools, the exhibitions, and the magazines and papers relating to the subject multiplied, a wealth of new ideas developed.

The artists of this period designed *all* forms of domestic articles. Entire rooms were decorated by what are now called interior decorators. Furniture, ceramics, glass, jewelry, posters, lamps, cutlery, anything you can think of was produced then, and every upper- or middle-class home was stuffed with vogue artifacts.

It was an eclectic fashion; classical, Renaissance, baroque, and rococo were all represented, and some of the designs may be traced to Celtic, Gothic, and Japanese art. Geoffrey Warren in his book, *The All Colour Book of Art Nouveau*, analyzes this tendency to include something of everything in every room. At its best the trend succeeded, he writes. "At its worst a whole room, particularly in the extreme Art Nouveau style, was too overwhelming and restless to be lived with."

The room we see here, from the author's collection, is, as are so many miniature rooms, a remembrance of someone known in childhood. The wicker pieces are all by Bob Bernhard of Dolphin Originals (see Appendix), and I doubt that they could be duplicated by anyone with less than Bernhard's expertise. The carpet, like the one in the preceding antebellum room, is an all-wool Brussels, and in the past few years there have been quite a few of these offered at sales and shows.

The Art Nouveau bedroom is distinguished by its stained-glass windows. Curves and whorls are embodied also in the cornices and frame. Portraits of Victoria and Albert hang above the bed and are offered already framed by Miniature Mart.

This bedroom set of the Art Nouveau period is by James Sweet. It is made of walnut, especially selected for its fine grain. All glass was cut by hand. Notice the brass shaving stand with brush on top of the chiffon robe and the brass casters on all the pieces that are movable.

They were quite the rage for adult-size rooms at the turn of the century and are perfect for this kind of miniature room.

The dressing table (vanity) at left and the wardrobe at right are part of a four-piece set made especially for the author by James Sweet of Santa Ana, California, exact copies from an illustration in a Sears, Roebuck catalogue of the period. It is made of solid walnut with walnut burls; the workmanship is fantastic. Notice that even the mirror was carved in flowing lines, all brasses were made by hand, and the shirt drawers in the wardrobe are exact to the last curve.

The little brass casters on the furniture were made of brass stripping ⅛″ wide; a piece ½″ long bent in two places to form a U. Quarter-inch brass pins were then slipped through holes drilled in the brass stripping, a ⅛″ wooden bead was slipped on, then the pins went through a hole in the other side, the excess was cut off, and the pins were soldered. In all of my miniatures, these casters seem to be the one thing that commands the most attention.

The "Staffordshire" groups shown here are imported by Mary Jane Graham. The workmanship is impeccable, and the colors make the pieces lovely accessories. Author's collection. (*Photograph by Sam Taylor*)

Figure 15
Tiffany Windows
for Art Nouveau Rooms

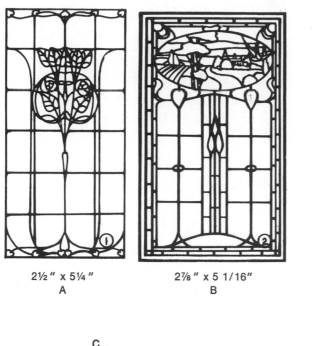

2½" x 5¼"
A

2⅞" x 5 1/16"
B

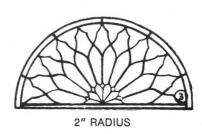

2" RADIUS

1⅛" x 3¼"

1 3/16" x 2 11/16"

C

1½" x 3 15/16"

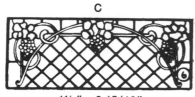

1" x 1½"

D

1" x 3½"   1 7/16" x 3½"

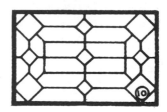

2" x 3"

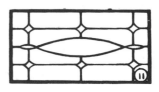

1 7/16" x 3"

TIFFANY LAMP SHADES

This charming little room is offered by Craft Patterns and Crafts Products Company, either finished or in kit form—or you can make your own from scratch with the pattern offered. Size is 15″ wide, 8″ deep, and 13½″ high. A hole has been cut in the back wall to accommodate a fireplace, and a window with panes has been framed with miniature molding.

Doreen Sinnett's module rooms measure 15″ wide, 11″ deep, and 10″ high and may be used either singly or in groups. The roofs make a charming finish for the rooms and give the effect of a complete house when the rooms are stacked.

This regency shop front by Bob Bern-hard is a fine subject for study, since so many of the principles for miniature rooms are used here. Note especially the purity of design and the lack of clutter in the arrangement. Photograph by Bob Bernhard.

This flower shop by Bob Bernhard demonstrates the effectiveness of dividing a miniature room in half to show both inside and outside. Notice how the eye is carried from the flowers on the sidewalk to those in the shop. Photograph by Bob Bernhard.

This artist's studio was one of the first miniature rooms made by John Blauer. A cat-and-dog fight has upset the room, spilling the contents of the artist's paint box. The intricate caning of the chairs was done by Helen Dorsett. Photograph by Craig Lund.

Interiors, walls, and doors of the Blauers' hat shop are made of construction board; the floral panels are available at decoupage shops. John made the figure from chenille pipe cleaners; tables, chairs, and display stands were made by Ellen. Hats are by Francille Hanson. Photograph by Craig Lund.

All silver pieces in this room are exact copies of those in the Smithsonian Institution. The El-Kru china pieces are made in the Blue Onion pattern, designed by Ellen Blauer; the oval pictures are, in reality, full-color postage stamps. The furniture represents the work of Betty Valentine, Edward Norton, Jean Kirkwood, and Elizabeth Zorn. Photograph by Craig Lund.

Detail of the colonial dining room shown above offers a closer look at the fine plaster work on the walls and the elegance of the furniture. Photograph by Craig Lund.

Dining room, suggested by the Gibbes-Sloan house and the Radcliff King house, is by Ellen and John Blauer. The setting is made principally of construction board. Gold-embossed die-cut paper was appliquéd to the crown molding to simulate the decoration of the original. Photograph by Craig Lund.

In this drawing room ca. 1800, created by Ellen and John Blauer, special note should be taken of the chess set in sterling silver-and-gold plate. The French scale on the fireplace, the tea set, and the delicate lyre clock were created by Ellen. Chairs are by Betty Valentine and Wes Faurot. Photograph by Craig Lund.

Bob Bernhard created this turn-of-the-century kitchen from a Maxwell Mays painting. The red panel at back center, while not authentic, is tremendously effective. Photograph by Bob Bernhard.

This Tudor room is constructed of black walnut panelling. While the portrait of Queen Isabella of Spain represents an earlier period, the Blauers, creators of the room, point out that Isabella was the mother of Catherine of Aragon and this setting represents Queen Catherine's sitting room. Photograph by Craig Lund.

Jim Weilepp's Gold Rush Bar demonstrates an ingenious use of space. The end of the box is utilized to carry the action out to the street and simultaneously provides a place to hook up electrical wiring. Everything in the room was made by Mr. Weilepp. Photograph by Sam Taylor.

The author's Japanese sitting room came about when a friend in Tokyo began to send back very special Japanese pieces. Sliding-screen walls were simple to construct; the scenes outside were made from magazine or book illustrations. Photograph by Sam Taylor.

This oil painting is representative of the fine work done by bona fide miniature room artists. Portrait was painted by W. Dee Burnett. Photograph by W. Dee Burnett.

Author's music room features carpets that were made from a Turkish prayer rug. Banjo and guitar made of Toledo ware (mother-of-pearl and gold) were originally brooches. The harp is a gift from the late Joseph Gray. Photograph by Sam Taylor.

In the author's colonial kitchen, boxes were extended from the back of the room to accommodate a fireplace and a staircase. Nearly everything here was made by the author. Photograph by Sam Taylor.

Apothecary shop, designed by John Blauer, has over seventy-five bottles on the shelves, each individually labeled. The working balance scale is from Joseph Gray. Photograph by Craig Lund.

Eugene Kupjack built the box for this sitting room, and Mary Jane Graham furnished it. Kupjack has used the windows, shelves, and arches to their greatest advantage. The box is 32″ wide, 12″ deep, and 10½″ high. Photograph by Jessie Walker Associates.

This French provincial country living room with beamed ceiling was built by Eugene Kupjack for Eunice Gold. The room is 27″ wide, 10″ deep, and 9″ high. The width includes a small outside garden with flowers growing in it. Identical flowers are included in the bowl at right. The shell motif on the fireplace mantel is repeated on both sides of the gaming table and on the lower doors of the breakfront. Photograph by James Kleinlenderink.

Miniature of the original Beehive Studio, where miniature rooms began in earnest. The box is 14″ wide and 8″ deep. The side walls and back scenes give the feeling of a room, rather than a vignette. Photograph by George Peterson.

A private theater was a fixture in many Victorian mansions. Notice how the eye is carried to the scene at stage rear. Many sets of scenery can be devised for a variety of productions. Author's collection. Photograph by Sam Taylor.

Art Nouveau bedroom, complete with brass bed. The heavy velvet cornices are typical of the period as are the dressing table and wardrobe by James Sweet. Carpet is a typical Brussels wool. Wicker furniture is by Bob Bernhard of Dolphin Originals. Note the stained glass windows. Author's collection. Photograph by Sam Taylor.

This version of a wickerware bedroom is dateless. All the wicker furniture is by Bob Bernhard, and the two chests in the rear are by Petite Princess. Author's collection. Photograph by Sam Taylor.

Exact copy of a sitting room in a house in Mechanicsburg, Pennsylvania, ca. 1865. Fabric covers the walls, the velvet upholstery is hand painted. Author's collection. Photograph by Sam Taylor.

A corner drugstore, ca. 1920. Notice that a corner is actually cut from the box and a column installed, as it was in the old days. The revolving fan in the center of the ceiling is by Amity Petites. The Tiffany fixtures are from Wee "C" Shop, Elmhurst, Illinois. Author's collection. Photograph by Sam Taylor.

This elegant foyer, built by Narcissa Thorne, is actually a vignette. The embrasure in the rear gives a feeling of space, which is not often achieved in such a small box. Photograph by Elinor Coyle.

Another foyer in the Regency period is opulently furnished with black marble walls and two busts on pedestals. The frame, which is exquisite, was especially made for the setting by Narcissa Thorne and her associates. Photograph by Elinor Coyle.

This bakery is patterned after one that still exists. Note the backlighting, which lends a dramatic effect to this room. Photograph by Gene Rose.

The detail in this general store is even more bewildering when one considers the fact that the fruit, vegetables, and other tiny objects were modeled to the ½″ scale. Everything in the room was made by Mrs. Pieroni. Photograph by Gene Rose.

A garden party in the Victorian manner. The background ties the front of
the box to the horizon and is fashioned from a piece of printed silk jersey.
Author's collection. Photograph by Sam Taylor.

Early July 4th picnics featured political speakers, and this one is no exception.
"Honest John Also Ran" is haranguing a family in the city park. The figures
are 1940 Renwal jointed plastic. Author's collection. Photograph by Sam Taylor.

I used a brass bed in this setting, however, rather than the bed made for the set; brass beds of every sort and shape were the vogue at the turn of the century, and in most middle-class homes furniture was inherited from a member of the family, so that rarely did any one room present a picture of exactly matched pieces.

Notice that the frame on the box and the cornice around the ceiling have been selected to repeat the flowing lines so much in vogue at this time. Even the family photos on the wall at left are framed in paper quilling because of the curved design (for paper-quilled frames, see *Make Your Own Dollhouses and Dollhouse Miniatures*). The little jewelry chest on the vanity bench is lined in black velvet and contains a rhinestone necklace and earrings, as well as a tiny wristwatch on a bracelet that would just about fit a ¼″ wrist!

Of special interest here, however, are the stained-glass windows on the back wall, executed by Lou Kummerow of Dollhouses (see Appendix). Kummerow seems to have his own technique for making these beautiful windows, and I know of no one else who can equal him. Some of his designs are shown (figure 15) but they have to be seen to appreciate the impact of the colors. These appear to be made on a base of clear resin or Mylar, placed over a sheet on which the design is drawn. The design is then traced (outlined) using LePage's liquid solder, but you must practice with this until you are able to draw out exactly the right bead of the solder to contain the color. Your hobby shop may have sets for making stained-glass windows; you might use one of these for practice.

The outline will harden in about an hour, and the coloring is then dropped with an eye dropper into the spaces designated. The resin will cure in about three hours, and it can then be pulled away from the paper backing. If your box is lighted from the back, the windows will shine like jewels.

Because of the elaborate furniture, I used simple net curtains here, many times washed to make them soft, with cornices constructed from the directions given in Chapter 7 and covered with red velvet. The actual room from which this design was taken also had side draperies made of red velvet, but in this small box they seemed to overpower everything else. They are much better omitted, for a finer material wouldn't give the voluptuous Art Nouveau effect.

Brass Bed

While the bed shown is a special design combining brass and iron, you might have some fun making the brass bed shown in figure 16, with which an enterprising miniaturist won first prize in the 1975 *Dollhouse and Miniature News* Originality Contest—a bed made from paper clips!

Mary Anne Conley wrote me, "I am employed as a secretary and I've often thought there *must* be something more interesting to be done with paper clips and other assorted office paraphernalia, and the attached two beds are what grew from my thinking. Bear in mind that this project can be as complex or as simple as the imagination or inclination of the craftsman dictates."

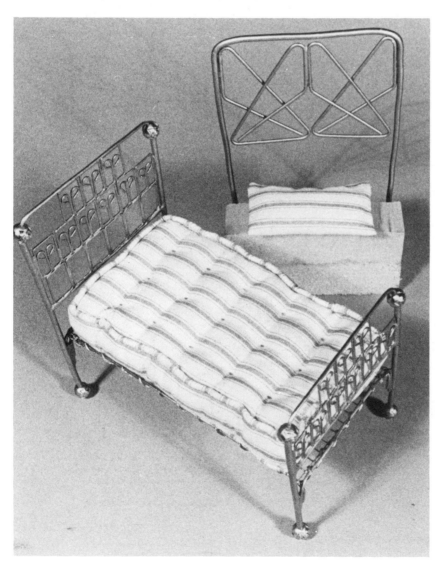

This brass bed, made from paper clips by Mary Anne Conley, won first prize in a contest staged by *Dollhouse and Miniature News.*

No. 2 paper clips, or 2 1⅝″ No. 1 paper clips, shaped as shown

8 rosebud beads, style 304 (Westrim Novelties)

4 1¼″ brads or nails of a diameter to fit snugly through bead and into the tubing

1 length ⅛″ copper tubing, about 18″ long

1 length No. 14 soft brass wire, about 40″ long

Thin wire such as used for pictures

Soldering iron, solder, and flux

Clamp

Needle-nosed pliers

Hacksaw for cutting tubing

Small file

Fine sandpaper

Small brush

Spray sealer, such as Royal Decoupage

Wire screen (hardware cloth)

Liquid solder (optional)

Treasure Brass (or any finish of your choice)

Assemble paper clips in three horizontal rows (she clipped the center section from the bottom row) and solder. Paper clips are slightly irregular in shape, so it helps to draw a straight line on the board or whatever you are soldering on to keep them lined up so your finished design won't lean to one side or waver. Solder the three rows together vertically and solder 3¼″ length of brass wire to the bottom (figure 16, *A*).

With a hacksaw, cut two pieces of copper tube 4½″ long and solder to the clips at their sides. Cut brass wire 5½″ long, bend with pliers as shown, and thread one bead at each end. Insert ends into the tube and solder the center to the top of the clips (figure 16, *B*). The footboard is constructed in the same manner as the headboard, using just the two top rows of the paper-clip design and cutting the side sections of tubing 3¼″ long. Cut two pieces of brass wire 4½″ long and two pieces 7¼″ long for the frame. Bend and solder to head and footboard as in figures 16, *C* and *D*. It helps to clamp the head and footboard sections to a board when you solder the frame sections, especially since you need to hold the side sections of the frame at a right angle to them.

Wash the bed gently with soap and water, and dry thoroughly. Finish each foot by inserting a nail through a bead and into the copper tubing. Use a hammer to tap the nail into the tubing; it should be a

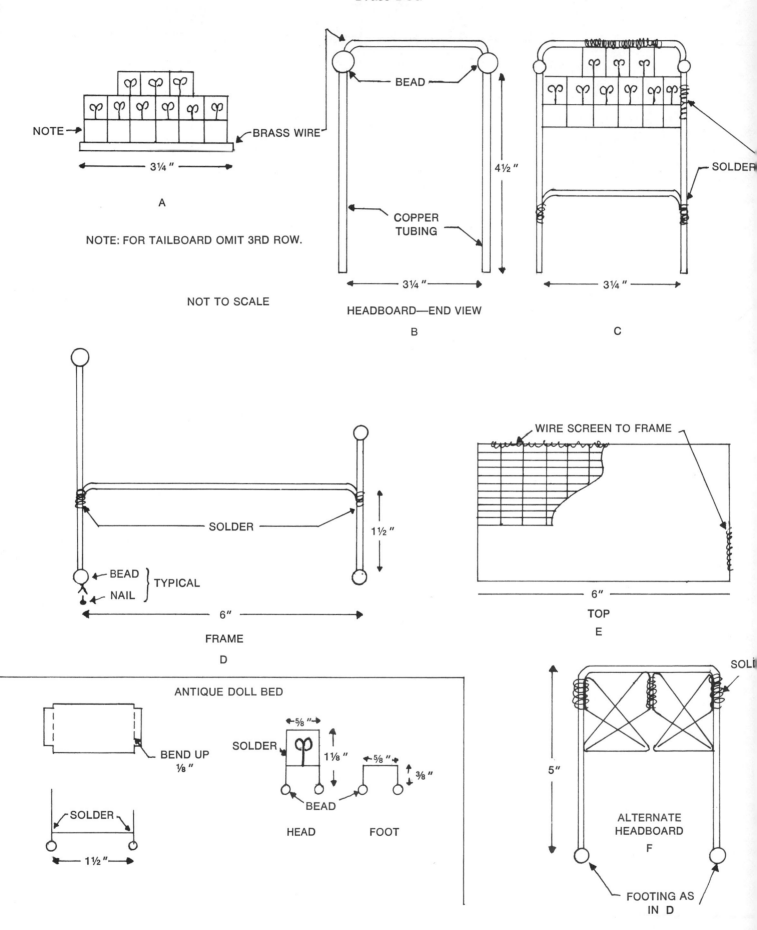

Figure 16
Brass Bed

NOTE → | BRASS WIRE
3¼"

A

NOTE: FOR TAILBOARD OMIT 3RD ROW.

NOT TO SCALE

BEAD
4½"
COPPER TUBING
3¼"

HEADBOARD—END VIEW

B

SOLDER
3¼"

C

SOLDER
BEAD } TYPICAL
NAIL
6"

FRAME

D

WIRE SCREEN TO FRAME
6"

TOP

E

ANTIQUE DOLL BED

BEND UP ⅛"

SOLDER
1½"

SOLDER
5⁄8"
1⅛"
BEAD
HEAD

5⁄8"
3⁄8"
FOOT

SOLi

5"

ALTERNATE HEADBOARD

F

FOOTING AS IN D

snug fit so that it won't slip out. A drop of liquid solder could be applied. If you can't find nails the right size, attach the beads with liquid solder (figure 16, D).

Finish with Treasure Brass. It can be applied slightly thinned, with finger or brush. Mary Anne used both methods. The bedspring is cut from hardware screen with tin snips or old scissors and wired to the frame with thin wire.

The assembly of the second headboard is somewhat simpler and shown in figure 16, F.

Mary Anne used a 42-watt iron, a ⅛" chisel tip, and 40/60 solid-wire solder that came with a tube of all-purpose flux advertised in the Sears, Roebuck catalogue. This wasn't the type of solder recommended (most articles specify 60/40), but it was the type Sears offered. And since she didn't know at the time the difference between 60/40 and 40/60, she purchased it in happy ignorance and it proved satisfactory.

Apply the flux to the pieces to be joined. Pick up a small amount of solder on the tip of the iron and apply it to the sections to be joined. Only a tiny drop is necessary to join the paper clips. When soldering the clips together, hold them down with the pliers, which won't conduct heat fast enough to burn your fingers. Slightly larger amounts of solder are applied to the area where the clips and frame are joined to the copper tubing, but use the same method. Wipe the tip frequently with a damp sponge.

Mary Anne reports that it's possible the liquid solder might work throughout the project, but she wasn't sure it would be strong enough. It does have the advantage of not requiring heat so you could manipulate small objects without danger of burning your fingers.

MATTRESS AND PILLOW

For materials, you will need a remnant or about ¼ yard narrow-stripe ticking fabric, thread, string, and stuffing. Cut two pieces of ticking, each 6¼" × 3½" (top and bottom). Cut two pieces of ticking, each 22" × 1" (welting). Cut one piece of ticking 22" × 1½" (sides). Cut two pieces string, each 22" long.

Fold the welting pieces in half lengthwise, wrong sides together, insert string, and, using a zipper foot, stitch close to the string. Trim to ¼".

Stitch welting to top and bottom of the side section, right sides together, raw edges even. Starting at one corner, join the side section to

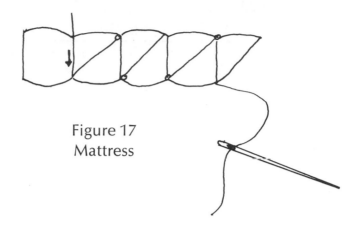

Figure 17
Mattress

the top, right sides together. Stitch in a ¼″ seam, clipping the side sections at the corners. Stitch the ends of the side sections together, cutting off the excess. Stitch the bottom of the mattress to the side section in the same manner, leaving one end open for stuffing. Turn and stuff and slipstich close.

Lightly mark the top and bottom of the mattress for simulated buttons. Using six-strand embroidery thread, sew, pulling the thread tight enough to plump up the mattress.

When you see the bed finished, you'll say it's worth all the trouble and more!

Art Nouveau Doll Bed

(see figure 16)

Materials Needed for This Project

1 No. 2 paper clip, shaped like those on the large bed
2 regular (1¼″) paper clips
1 tin can
  Narrow paper trim (type used for decoupage)
4 small gold beads, style 2455/3 (Westrim Novelties)
  Liquid solder
  Soldering iron, solder, and flux
  Treasure Brass and sealer
1 scrap of fleece
1 scrap of lace

Cut a 1¾″ × ¾″ piece from the tin can, snip ⅛″ corners out, and then bend the ends up. Straighten the 1¼″ paper clips, and cut one piece 3″ long for the head of the bed and one piece 1½″ long for the foot. Bend as illustrated. Then solder the No. 2 paper clip to the top of the headboard. Solder head and foot to the ends of the tin-can piece. Cut a decoupage strip to fit around the sides of the bed and glue the ends with liquid solder. Insert the feet into the gold beads. Finish with the Treasure Brass and spray with sealer. Glue the piece of fleece on for a mattress; use the scrap of lace for the coverlet.

The bed that actually belongs to the set in this room is pictured with the other two pieces on page 84. Here the bow ends of the bed are seen as well as the walnut-burl inlays. The bedspread is hand loomed from Chestnut Hill, but in my estimation the rich silk and velvet crazy quilt (see *Make Your Own Dollhouses and Dollhouse Miniatures*) is much more appropriate for this room. The elegant little "Staffordshire" figures are obtainable only from It's a Small World (see Appendix); they are imported from England by Mary Jane Graham and are of superb quality and quite inexpensive. The larger ones shown here are about 1″ tall, the smaller ranging from ½″ to a bit larger. Colors and workmanship are exquisite.

The little slippers on the floor at the front of the box are from Sylvia Rountree of the Dolls' Cobbler (see Appendix) and are perfect for hinting at the presence of a member of the family, as are the stereoscope and diary on the chaise longue as well as the hand-carved wooden tea set from Mexico on the table at right.

Art Nouveau Shaving Stand

This little project was also an entry in the 1975 Originality Contest of *Dollhouse and Miniature News*. It is the creation of Barbara Bruton of Dallas, Texas. You can see it atop the chifforobe in the photo of Jim Sweet's bedroom set.

Materials Needed for This Project
- 1 wooden bead, ½″ in diameter
- 1 round mirror, ½″ in diameter
- 1 flat head brass pin, 1 1/16″ long
- 1 gold filigree bead cap, ⅜″ diameter, 3/16″ deep, No. B38 (Make It Happen Craft Studio)
- 1 gold-metal filigree finding, ⅝″ diameter (before flattening), No. 1718 (Craft House)
- 1 small scrap of toilet soap
  LePage's liquid solder glue
  Gold paint

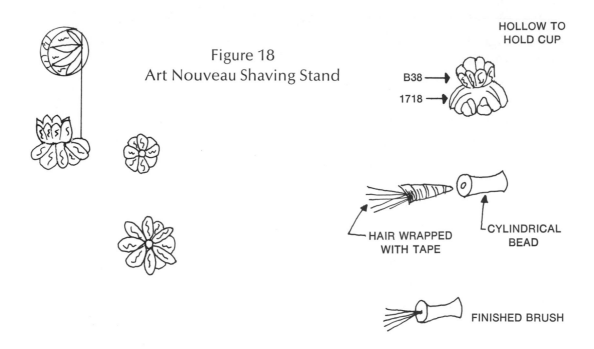

Figure 18
Art Nouveau Shaving Stand

HOLLOW TO HOLD CUP

B38 →

1718 →

HAIR WRAPPED WITH TAPE

CYLINDRICAL BEAD

FINISHED BRUSH

Cylindrical gold finished bead, ⅛″ × ¼″ with longitudinal shaft
A few strands hair from an old wig
Magic mending tape
Elmer's glue

Since the No. 1718 gold-metal filigree findings are convex-concave, gently flatten one using a ½″ wooden bead. Center the ½″ mirror on the flattened finding and gently crimp the edge of the finding up around the edge of the mirror to frame it. Again using the wooden bead, gently shape another of the No. 1718 filigree findings so that it becomes a shallow bowl. This piece then serves as the base of the stand. Place a dot of the liquid solder glue in the center hole of the base and center the No. B38 bead cap on the base so that their center holes are concentric. Allow glue to dry.

Cut a flatheaded brass pin to a length of 1 1/16″ and insert it through the base. The upright pin will serve as the post to hold the mirror. Apply a dab of the liquid solder glue to the pinhead (which is under the base) so that it will be held securely in place against the base. Make sure that the pin is properly supported during drying so that it is perpendicular to the bottom of the finished stand.

On the front side, apply the liquid solder glue along the tip of the pin down about ¼″. Apply a dot of the glue to the center hole of the back of the framed mirror and apply the framed mirror to the upright brass pin. Secure on a block of wood so that when dry the mirror will be straight. Allow the glue to dry. Using a very small brush, cover liquid solder with gold paint.

The shaving brush is constructed from a cylindrical bead with longitudinal bore and a tuft of hair from an old wig. Enlarge the hole in one end of the bead by inserting and gently twisting an awl in the hole. Cut a small tuft of hair from an old wig and bind it at the cut end with tape, wrapping diagonally so as to have a small free end of tape wrapped around itself to form a point. Insert the pointed end of the tape into the enlarged hole in the bead. Adjust for fit. Cut off any excess tape after removing the hair from the bead. Apply Elmer's glue to the taped end and reinsert.

This clever woman bought her findings from the Make It Happen Craft Studio, 2620 B West Chester Pike, Broomall, Pennsylvania 19008.

Chandelier

Lucille Spinka of Riverside, Illinois, one of the foremost miniaturists in the country, designed this chandelier for her own dollhouse. Appropriate for almost any room of the late Victorian or Art Nouveau periods (notice the curling leaves and flowers, both of which are characteristics of these periods), it is a joy to make and lovely to behold.

Here are the instructions for a four-light working chandelier with simulated gas jets in a vine-and-rose motif. To make one with fewer or more lights, it is only necessary to determine the number desired and evenly space the arms around the central point.

Materials Needed for This Project

1 length soft brass tubing, .090" OD
1 length soft brass tubing, .125" OD
   Tubing bender or grooved ½" dowel
   Tubing cutter or fine-toothed jeweler's saw
   Small screwhead countersink
1 flat-back filigree medallion-type jewelry finding, 30 to 60 mm, to be used as ceiling plate
2 30-mm flat-back stone settings with swedge holes, center hole not more than ⅛"
4 pearlized white plastic rings
4 gold bell caps
4 miniature lamps with attached wires (Illinois Hobbycraft)

1 length 24 or 26 gauge insulated wire, 18″ long

G.E. Silicone Seal

Brass paint

Aron-Alpha or Krazy glue

Epoxy glue

Florist's wire

Bread dough for making roses, or flowers removed from old jewelry

Plastic doily

Cut one piece of the .125″ tubing about 1/16″ shorter than the overall height you want your chandelier to be. You will have to adjust the height to your room dimensions. Solder (or cement) one end to the

This Art Nouveau chandelier by Lucille Spinka is appropriate for either Victorian or Art Nouveau rooms. (*Photograph by James Klein Lenderink*)

A fascinating variety of chandeliers is available to the maker of miniature rooms. The first three at left are by Ellen Blauer of Miniature Mart; next a hand-blown creation made to order for the author. Center, a crystal chandelier by Willoughby's 18th Century. At far right, a Tiffany shade by Lou Kummerow. Second from right, a Victorian fixture from Shackman. Third from right, a crystal-bead chandelier by the author.

ceiling plate. To the other end solder or cement one of the stone settings with the open side down. This will be the stem with the ceiling plate and one half of the "junction box" (the place where all the wires will connect).

Next, form the arms from the .090″ tubing by bending the ends of the full length to a 90-degree angle. Make sure not to kink the tube. This is best done with a small tubing bender; however, we used a grooved ½″ dowel rod to make the bends. The tubing may be cut best in a vise, with a tubing cutter or with a fine-toothed jeweler's saw.

Now cut the tube 1″ back from the center of the hole in the bent end. This will give you two arms about 1″ long for a chandelier having about a 3″ spread across the arms. Now repeat the bending and cutting procedure from the remaining piece of .090″ tubing to give you the necessary four arms. The inner edges must be reamed to eliminate sharp corners, which would cut through the insulation of the wires. A small screwhead countersink is ideal for this purpose, or, as a last resort, your fingernail file. Just twist the pointed end firmly in the hole.

The remaining stone mounting should have a turned-up, perforated filigree edge. Find four openings that are equally spaced around the edge and check to see if the straight ends of the arms will enter. If not, the openings may be enlarged with a round file, or if you have a Moto-Shop, a small rotary file will do it in a jiffy. Fit the arms exactly as you want them; that is, the straight end goes into the stone mounting

Figure 19
Basic Construction for Wired Chandelier

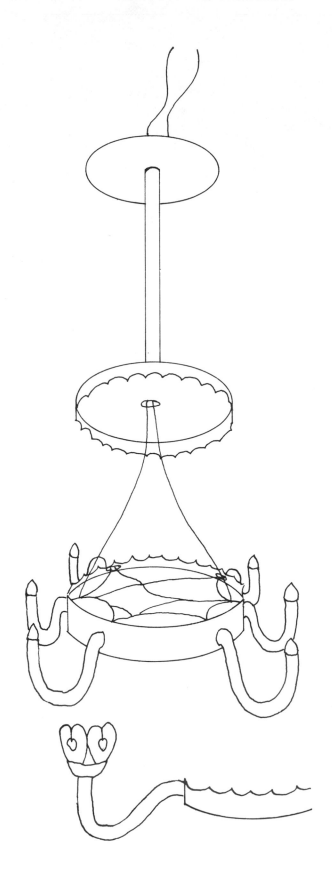

about ⅛″ with the prongs of the mounting up and the butt end of the tube also up. Set one at a time using a tiny bit of Aron-Alpha or Krazy glue to hold them in place. Since this dries very quickly, the arm can be held in place while it sets.

When the four arms are glued in place, let them "set up" for a bit and then do a permanent gluing job with Epoxy to strengthen the bond.

Next, cement the plastic rings into the bell caps. Form the caps up and around the rings with your fingers first; just press the sides up making sure that the bottom holes are centered. Glue together lightly. Glue these assemblies to the ends of the arms leaving about ¹⁄₁₆″ of tubing sticking up through the bottom of the cap-and-shade assembly.

When these subassemblies are thoroughly dry, you are ready for the wiring. Take each of the lamps and push the pair of "pigtails" (wires) through the arms from the cup end so that you will have four pairs of wires coming into the stone mounting, which now becomes a junction box. A very small amount of Epoxy glue at the base of the lamp will set it permanently straight on the arm. Strip ¼″ of insulation from the end of each wire and join one of each pair of wires together. This should give you two groups of four wires each—one wire from each lamp going to one group and the other wire from each lamp to the other group. Now take two 9″ lengths of about 24 or 26 gauge insulated wire and join one to each of the groups of four. This will give you two groups of five wires each. These connections must be soldered.

Before soldering, connect the two long wires to a 12-volt transformer to check the lamps and connections. They should all light. Try tapping the fixture lightly here and there; if you have a flicker, there is a poor connection somewhere. It must be found now and corrected. It is a good precaution to test each lamp for a short time before wiring it into the fixture.

When this is done, the two five-wire soldered joints must be well insulated. For this, use G.E. Silicone Seal. Be generous with it to make sure that all bare wire and solder are well covered. Pack the wires down into the lower half of the junction box so that the other half will close down tightly. Be careful not to rub the insulation from the wires.

When the insulation is dry, draw the two long wires through the stem and join the two halves of your junction box by either crimping the edges or gluing lightly with Epoxy.

This completes the base chandelier, electrically lighted. To make it appear gas lighted, simply add a chimney to each of the lamp cups.

These are available in several styles from Glassblower's Workshop (see Appendix).

When making an unlighted chandelier, eliminate the wiring and substitute 12 or 14 gauge bare soft copper wire instead of brass tubing. Stripped 12 or 14 gauge TW wire (electrical) is ideal, using the 12 gauge for the stem.

In the photograph you'll see a motif of rose vines on a typical mid-Victorian ornate brass six-light working chandelier. Thin florist's wire was wrapped around each stem from the bottom of the cup to the center post and secured with Epoxy. Another length was loosely wrapped from the ceiling plate to the base and glued in place.

Simple bread roses might be used for ornamentation, or you may have some appropriate small plastic flowers removed from old costume jewelry available. These are applied at random on the base, stem, and all arms of the chandelier with Super glue. Cut apart the leaves on the findings, making some of the stems short and leaving others a bit longer.

Beautiful little Art Nouveau desk piece in stained glass found in a department store measures 5″ × 7″ and will be used for large windows on stair landings. Note the inscription, "Gather ye rosebuds while ye may."

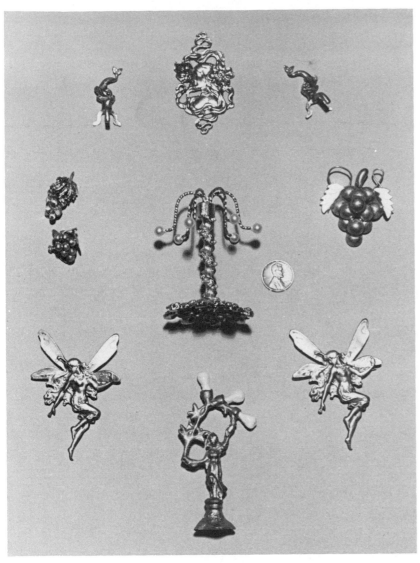

Many artifacts in Art Nouveau designs are found today. Center, a piece designed to hold rings but used on a newel-post in a 1900s room. Bottom, a piece used beside the proscenium arch in the theater. Top, and left and right of bottom, pewter pins and pendant with perfect Art Nouveau design. Next upward, earrings and pin with the Art Nouveau touch. Small pieces at top are dolphin andirons from Dolphin Originals.

Glue these in the same manner uniformly on the florist's wire that forms the vine down the stem and arms. You may want to glue some on the ceiling plate and junction box.

When all the leaves and roses are placed exactly as you would like them, go back and glue all contact places with Epoxy. This will give a permanent bond, and you will take no chances of anything loosening or falling off the fixture when you wire it into place in your room.

When all glue is dry, paint the entire fixture except the pearlized rings and bulbs with a good quality brass paint and wire into the room.

The center of a plastic doily was used for the ceiling medallion. Just glue on, cover with gesso, and paint the entire ceiling the color you want.

9 Private Theater

The thrills that come to you in the developing of your miniature rooms will reach a peak in this effort, the miniature theater.

The little theater is a joy to work on and to behold. It was copied from an unbelievable sight I was privileged to see one night. A friend who had bought the property of the old Lemp Brewing Company in St. Louis invited me to descend deep into the earth to see the cooling caves, where some of the huge casks of beer were still standing in the racks along the stone walls. Tucked into an enclosure in one of the caves was a room where an entire theater had been built. The scenery was still set on the 15' stage, the little footlights were still arrayed at the edge, and a dozen or so chairs were still there, some of them overturned, so that now, more than seventy-five years later, one could imagine these stout tycoons of St. Louis's greatest industry inviting the groups of players or dancing ensembles recruited from the beer halls to entertain their friends. In the steamy St. Louis summers, the fifty-degree temperature in the caves must have been most welcome, and it's easy to imagine the torrid parties that must have taken place there.

I decided to use the same-size box as others I had built—20″ × 11″ × 12″—since we wanted the boxes uniform for display purposes. Guy R. Williams, in his book *Making a Miniature Theater* (now long out of print) opts for a larger base—24″ wide × 15″ deep × 20″ high—but I like mine better. Once you've decided on the size, you have one more important decision to make. Williams uses the whole space for his stage. I felt that since a miniature theater such as we are making is a whole setting, an entity in itself, we must have a stage plus space for the audience to sit within the box. Decide for yourself. If you decide to have the entire box used as a stage, it is a simple matter to adjust my measurements to your space.

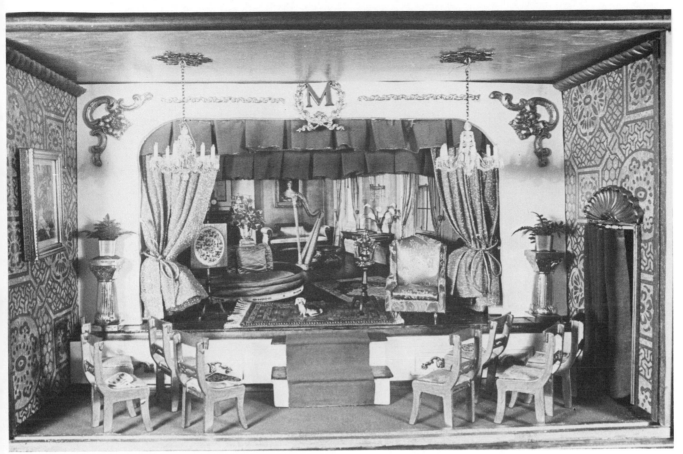

Completed stage with ceiling in place and two crystal chandeliers mounted. Here the backdrop is a book illustration. Notice that the point at which the stage meets the backdrop is barely apparent. The Turkish rug, chair, table, and fire screen are on the stage; borne and harp are in the background photo.

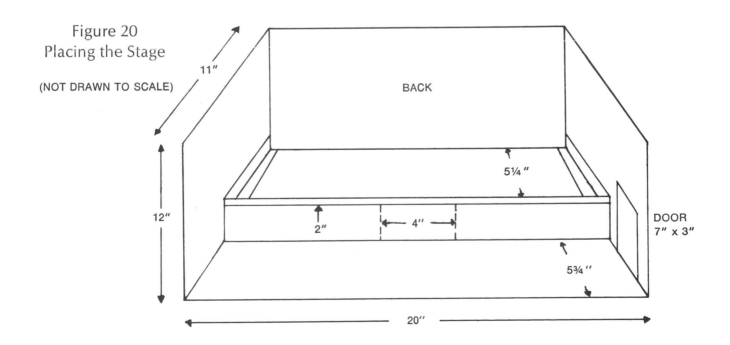

Figure 20
Placing the Stage

(NOT DRAWN TO SCALE)

11″

BACK

12″

5¼″

2″

4″

DOOR
7″ x 3″

5¾″

20″

Materials Needed for This Project

1 miniature box room, 20″ × 11″ × 12″ high, made of ⅜″ plywood, with lid

1 length 1″ balsa wood, 36″ long, for stage base

1 piece ⅜″ plywood, 18″ × 5¼″, for stage floor

1 piece veneer, 18″ × 5¼″, for stage-floor finish

1 length 1″ × 4″ balsa wood, 3″ long, to be cut for steps

2 pieces ⅛″ balsa wood, 1¼″ × 4⅛″, for step treads

2 pieces ⅜″ plywood, 9¾″ × 19⅞″, for prosceniums

1 piece ⅛″ mat board for various scenics

1 piece velveteen, ⅓ yard long, for carpet and curtain

1 piece velveteen, lamé, or metallic cloth, ⅓ yard long, for house curtain

Various fittings for decorating outside proscenium

White enamel

Gold paint

Decoupage glaze

Wallpaper of your choice for side walls

Brick wallpaper for back wall

1 length 1″ × 1″ balsa wood, 12″ long, for scene braces

Glue

8 plain chairs, to be gilded and upholstered

Various scenes for backdrops

2 light fixtures with medallions for ceiling

1 length ornate molding, 12″ long, for ceiling-wall joint

1 length ⁵⁄₃₂″ cove molding, 42″ long, for stage and floor

1 length baseboard, 10″ long, for walls

Lumber for door framing

Cut 1″ balsa wood into 2″-wide boards to build up the stage; the dimensions are shown in figure 20. Glue the sides to the front with butt joints, measuring before you glue; you should have a very snug fit. This is the foundation for the stage; the open space will take the electrical connections. Cut a piece of ⅜″ plywood 2″ shorter than this stage base and 5¼″ wide. This is the floor of the stage (figure 20). Veneer the stage floor in the wood and design you prefer, and finish. Wallpaper the back of the room and the sides up to the front of the stage with brick wallpaper; in all theaters these walls are left in the rough brick.

Making the stage 5¼″ deep leaves us 5¾″ for the front, or parquet, part of the theater. Eight pretty chairs of the sort sold by Shackman for dining-room chairs (but reupholstered and gilded) will fit

104

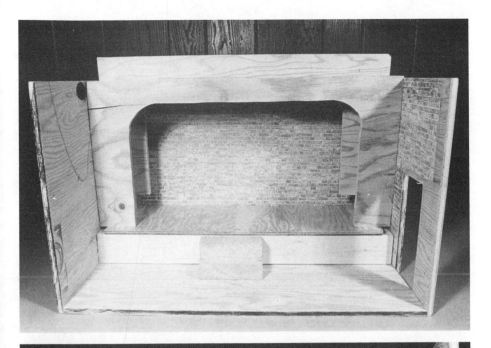

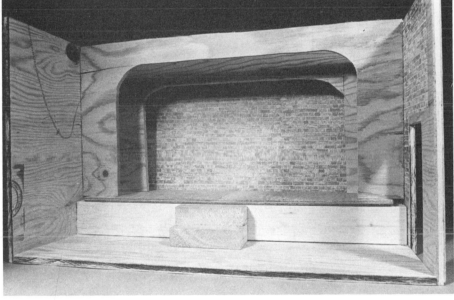

First stages in building the private theater are shown here. Top, the back stage of the proscenium arch is being slipped into place; bottom, both stages are ready for decoration and draping. Notice that the back and side walls have been papered with brick wallpaper as all back walls of a theater are always left in unfinished brick.

nicely into this space, and this number would just about take care of the group that the dollhouse family is inviting for an evening of fun.

You must have some way for the actors to reach the stage. I decided to build two steps in the center, made from pieces of 1″ balsa wood, one cut 2″ high and another cut 1″ high, both 4″ wide. Glue the 1″ piece against the 2″ piece and you have two steps. Paint the steps white. Cut two pieces ⅛″ balsa ¼″ deeper than the steps and ⅛″ wider. Stain and finish carefully (see the instructions for finishing floors in Chapter 6). Glue these to the top of the steps even with the back.

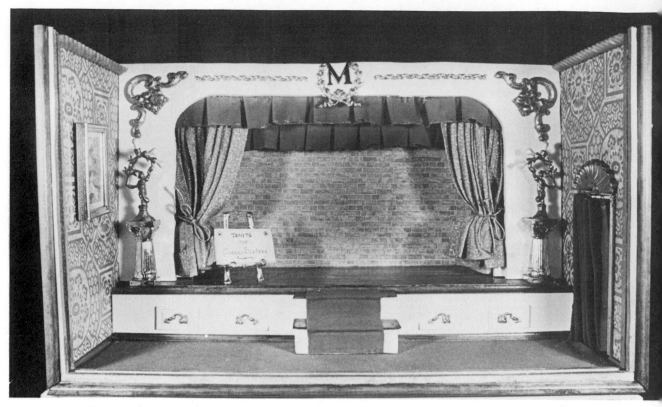

Proscenium treatment shows decoration at the front of the stage, wallpaper and door treatment in the front of the box. Figures at the side of the stage are lead painted gold, mounted on gold risers ordinarily used on wedding cakes.

Now, we must have decorations for that bare front of the stage. You may wish to make your own panels; I purchased the No. EW201B Georgian panels from the Miniature Mart (see Appendix) and glued them to the front of the stage as shown in the photos. Glue to the front of the stage, then give everything two coats of white enamel. I then applied tiny brass ornaments to the center of each panel; you might use No. H2383, No. J9743, or No. J206 from the Miniature Mart. Give each a coat of decoupage glaze after the glue is dry to prevent the brass from darkening.

The walls of your theater will need some thought. If you'll recall some theaters you have seen, you'll remember plaster walls with lots of rococo gold decoration. We need a lot of gold in a theater; we want a sparkling, alive room. Plain rough white with a lot of filigree applied would be fine. I chose to use a gold wallpaper, a copy of an old tea-chest paper that I have in my living room, for these walls. Paper back to behind the curtains to meet the brick walls. With the paper in place, you can slide your stage in.

For the parquet or seating area in front of the stage, I veneered the floor (and it looked very well) but then found a remnant of brilliant red velveteen, which I promptly installed as a carpet. But I didn't fasten it down, since I felt I might want to change it later. With the carpet in place, I glued the steps in place in the center of the stage. Choose a tiny curved molding (Northeastern's $\frac{5}{32}''$ cove molding is exactly right) and glue in place over the carpet at the stage and along the top of the stage facing at the edge of the stage floor. Glue the baseboard strips along the sides of the seating space. Paint the door trim gold and glue in place, together with an ornament over the door.

Time to place a red velvet curtain in the doorway. Measure the velveteen or other material to the exact height of the door opening. Make it double the width of the opening. For this particular project I liked the method of gluing to aluminum foil the best. Cut a piece of lightweight foil the same size as the material and spray lightly with spray glue. Press on the material. Turn over and spray the other side and press on another piece of material, the same size. This will dry immediately. Trim the edges so they're neat and sharp; then run a thin line of any glue that dries clear along all four sides and allow to dry. Fold the side edges back upon themselves about $\frac{1}{4}''$. Mold some pleats around a pencil; you don't want sharp creases, but a soft effect. It's surprisingly easy to do. You'll have five or six pleats plus the end fold-overs, so you must have seven or eight small rings from your hobby shop, about $\frac{1}{4}''$ in diameter. Tack these lightly to the back side of the pleats.

Cut a $\frac{1}{8}''$ dowel so that it fits very snugly in the door opening; paint it gold and let dry. Here, we encounter one of the most puzzling anomalies of miniature making. I have experimented for years, trying to make tiny fixtures to attach to the inside of doorways upon which rods could be hung, but I have never found a satisfactory solution. In most cases, you have only a $\frac{3}{8}''$ square to work with. It will split if you try to make a hole for the rod in it. Any metal used looks homemade. In this case, because there would be little weight on the rod, I just cut a tight fit with the $\frac{1}{8}''$ dowel, threaded the dowel through the rings on the curtain, put a dab of glue on the ends of the rod, and then forced it into the doorway and pushed up against the top of the opening. It stayed.

You will have seen some theaters where the door curtains were looped back with gold cords, and if you want this effect, use just one thickness of the material, glue the hems in place, and then attach rings

Cake dividers shown come in white, gold, and silver; heights 10″, 6″, and 4″, from Maid of Scandinavia. They have many uses in room building. The small one at far right has been stained walnut for a Victorian room.

as above. Tie back with gold cord. It has a tendency to look clumsy, though.

For your proscenium arches, you will need two pieces of the ⅜″ plywood the exact length of your stage and the height of your box measured from the stage floor. In my case, this was 9¾″ high by 19⅞″ long. For the front arch, mark off 2½″ at each side and 1⅜″ down from the top. For the back, or second, arch, mark off 3″ at the sides and 2½″ down from the top. Sketch in your arches as shown in figure 21 until you have the curves at the corners exactly right; then cut out the centers. If you have a Dremel Moto-Shop, this will do the sawing exactly and quickly. If you have no Dremel, a jeweler's saw (about $7.00) or

Figure 21
Proscenium Arches

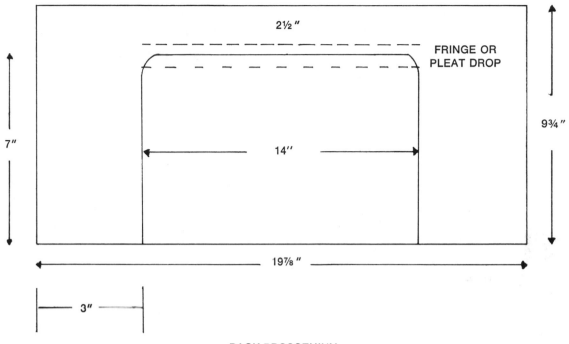

BACK PROSCENIUM

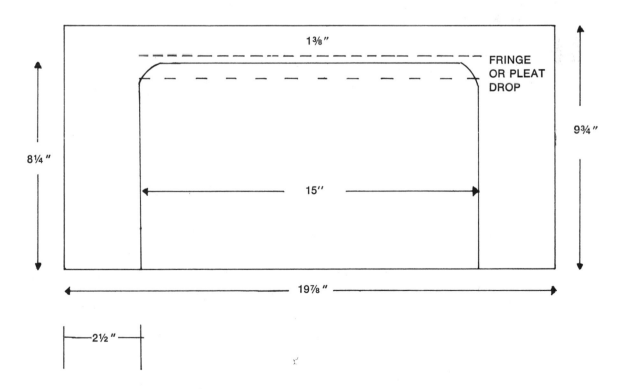

FRONT PROSCENIUM

coping saw (about $3.50) will do a fine job for you and come in handy for many other jobs. Paint the front of the arches or cover with a dark-ish material, which is what is used in some theaters. The front arch would be covered with the darker material, the back with the lighter. On a stage, colors lighten from front to back to carry the eye backward. I painted the back arch white and the front arch a light pearl gray and found this very satisfactory.

Curtains and Draperies

The simplest top curtains for our miniature arches is a drop of fringe. Buy a yard of 2″ silk fringe in gold or the color you prefer. Cut it in half, and glue one half to the top of the inner proscenium, right at the edge. Glue the other half to the inside top of the outer proscenium, also right at the edge.

Another possibility for these "ceiling drops," if you cannot find fringe that is heavy enough to be impressive, is to use the same vel-veteen used for the floor and door. Cut a strip 1½″ wide and twice as long (allowing an extra 2″ to go behind the arch on each side) for each arch. On your pressing board over a Turkish towel, pin this piece into box pleats about 1″ apart, with the velvet side down. Press the pleats in with a steam iron or iron and moist cloth. When the pleats are in, fasten at the top with a row of machine stitching as close as possible to the top, or with staples. To finish the bottom edge, tip with a line of any good glue that dries clear; this cannot be done before pressing, for the glue will melt. Allow to dry; then gently push the pleats into place.

Just behind this will go the "house curtain," which would be the curtain the audience sees before the play begins (the one that in vaude-ville days carried all the advertising signs). But you must remember that we have only some 5″ of space to work with. So I did without the house curtain and erected a movable curtain that could be drawn back and forth but which I kept secured at the sides as shown in the photo. This must be made of some rich and impressive material. Velvet is ideal but very bulky in such a small space unless it is chiffon velvet. If you use this, don't sew the hems in; merely trace with a line of glue and let dry; then trim. I happened to have an old cocktail blouse of gold lamé that was just the right weight; that's what you see in the photo. A heading is made at the top and the curtain is slipped onto a ⅛″ dowel 18″ long. It hangs on two shoulder hooks (the smallest you can find) that are screwed in just over the fringe at the back of the arch. Tie the curtains back from their drop with gold cord, as high or as low as you think is realistic. Hook the tie-backs onto upholstery tacks with fancy heads that have been tapped into the edge of the arch.

Decoration of the outer proscenium arch must be very elaborate and ornamental. Notice that I have used wood embossed corners, such as both Constantine's and Craftsman Wood Service carry, and painted them gold. Other decorations on the arch are just dribs and drabs of material found in my box and painted gold. The *M* at the top of the arch is a letter found in a discount hardware store for twenty-two cents; it supplies a personal note and a great deal of "class," I thought.

Now set up your stage, but don't glue the arches into place yet; we want to be certain that everything fits. Notice that the sides of the front arch look bare; almost any sort of decoration will go in here, but I liked best of all the little pedestals you see in the photo. These are very inexpensive and come in gold, silver, or white from Maid of Scandinavia (see Appendix). They could be topped with statuary, ferns, or

Stage with backdrop set for the street scene where Jack goes to town to sell the cow, from *Jack and the Beanstalk*. Notice that proper perspective in the backdrop carries the eye up and away to give an illusion of depth.

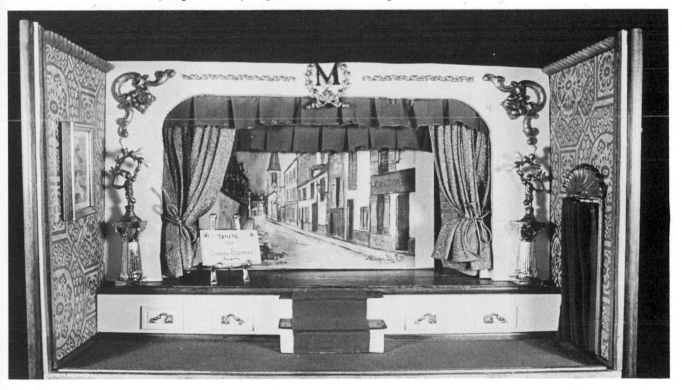

bouquets of flowers, depending upon the entertainment to be presented.

You will need backdrops; start looking for photos or scenes that you may mount on ⅛″ mat board. The one shown in our photo is an interior from an old home in one of the Richard Pratt series, *Treasuries of Early American Homes* (McGraw-Hill Book Company, 1946); it spread over two pages in the book; I removed it carefully and attached the left piece to the right. This was then mounted on the mat board in two pieces also, so that it could be bent at the back. It gave us a fine backdrop for the second act of *School for Scandal*.

I then needed a couple of wing sets, or "returns" (a return is a side flat, side curtain, or wing that runs parallel to the proscenium line; by varying the distance between a pair of returns the actual size of the stage opening can be manipulated). But rather than using scenery flats, I used, as may be seen, a fire screen on one side and an upholstered chair with table on the other. A small (5″ × 7″) petit-point Turkish rug was then laid on the stage floor; this further brings the eye down from the backdrop to the edge of the stage but leaves plenty of room for the dolls, who will be the players.

In the second photo, a scene set for *April in Paris* has a backdrop cut from a French wallpaper that I happened to have in the house. The wing flats are made from trees cut from the wallpaper, mounted on ⅛″ mat board and made to stand upright by gluing a 2″-long piece of 1″-square balsa wood to the base at the back. In a real theater, these flats would be "flied" from beams in the ceiling, but for our purpose, standing flats are much simpler and easier to handle. Use your imagination a bit and see what you can dream up, or find illustrations for.

Try to bring the scene forward by placing some actual set pieces on the stage. In the first photo, I have used the chair, table, and little dog. In the second, I've used a bench, a doll, and a cat. These things give life to the scene.

In a real theater, there is a "cloth," a rectangular sheet of canvas that hangs from a beam called a "batten." In our delineation, however, a cloth is easily made from paper or light cardboard, and it can either be mounted on mat board as described above and then braced from the back with a 1″-square piece of wood, or it can be hung from the roof on a length of ⅛″ wood that rests on the two prosceniums and the back wall. We show in our drawing a "cutcloth," which substitutes for a pair of wings and a border. It is easily made in the manner described above, and it's great for giving an irregular profile or reproducing rocks and trees.

Here's another example of the use of the backdrop to establish perspective. This setting is for the third act of *April in Paris*. The backdrop is made from a French wallpaper with a road leading away from the eye at an angle. Two movable side wings are cut from the wallpaper and mounted on mat board. The bench is painted green, and the floor covering is artificial grass.

A "border" is a cloth or flat arranged so that it appears to provide a ceiling for the stage. Two are shown. The builder should remember that the *downstage* (closest to the audience) border should have richer and stronger colors than the border nearer the backdrop.

Figure 22 shows borders for the forest scene from Hansel and Gretel. *A* is shaded darker at bottom and medium light at top for downstage; *B* is lighter in comparison and is for behind the back proscenium. We see in *C* a cutcloth made from paper mounted on mat board; sketch in tree trunks and tree leaves and set behind the borders. All three are glued onto 1/16″ sticks or dowels to hang from the top of the room sides.

Figure 22
Borders and Cutcloth

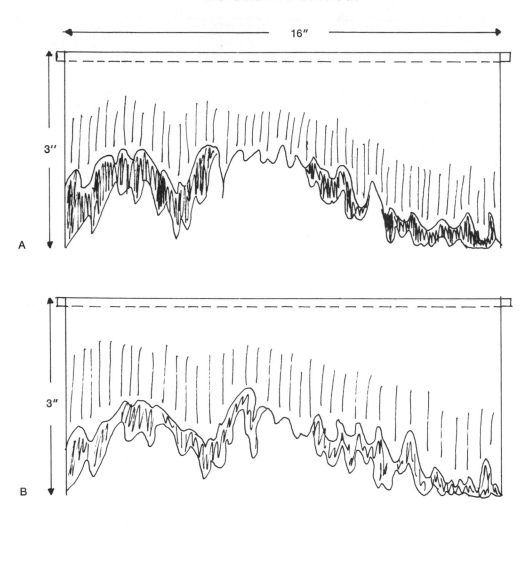

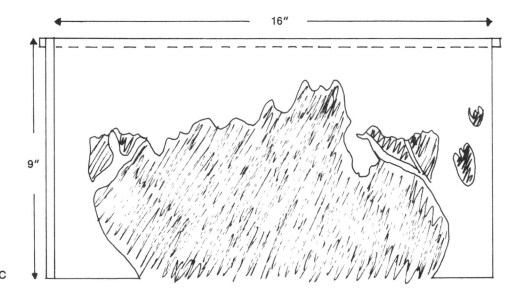

**FOR CUTCLOTH
CUT OUT SHADED PORTIONS**

Theater for the Dollhouse

One of the most interesting developments of the miniature theater is a tiny theater for the dollhouse, conceived by Charles Claudon of the drama department of Northwestern University.

Claudon explains that during the late Victorian and Edwardian eras, thousands of children entertained themselves with Pollock's toy theaters. They were sold "a penny plain and twopence coloured." They were made of cardboard and wood, and with the theater the buyer received all the sets, accessories, characters, and playbook for an entire production. The one shown is based on the Regency production (first published in 1834) of *Aladdin; or, The Wonderful Lamp.*

Claudon used a 1¾" scale for his tiny masterpiece to make it larger and more workable; his sketches are shown full size, so that you need only trace them from the page and then onto your mat board. Also, the originals were printed in bright colors, such as bright red, orange, and green, but he toned the colors down a bit on his reproduction, so they would seem better in the day nursery. The theater won third prize in the 1975 Originality Contest staged by *Dollhouse and Miniature News.*

Materials Needed for This Project

No. 2 pencil (not too soft)
Illustration board, ⅟₁₆" thick
Poster board, one side flat finish
Watercolors and fine paintbrushes.
Utility knife or razor blade
White glue

Trace items *A, B, C, D, E,* and *F* on the illustration board. Trace items *G, H, I, J,* and *K* onto the poster board. After tracing the items, either pencil or ink in the details (use waterproof ink). Paint the pieces.

These suggestions might be of help to you: *A, C, D,* and *G* make up the physical theater, so they are painted together. Claudon's proscenium (*A*) is pale green and light ocher, with a deep gold band bordering the false curtains. *B, E,* and *F* may be left white or painted the same as *A.*

H is a drop representing the interior of the cave. He painted the edges light gold and the rest a pale slate grey.

I represents the mouth of the cave, with a waterfall. Paint the shrubs green, the waterfall at right pale blue, the rocks on the floor pink, the rocks at right pale yellow, and the twisted rock pillar and remaining rocks should be painted variations of slate grey.

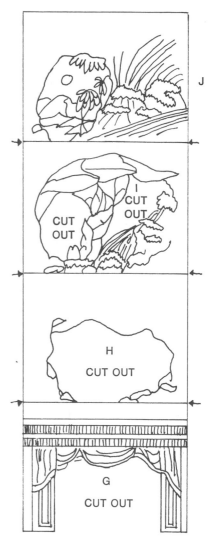

Figure 23
Toy Theatre

The completed stage for the dollhouse may be judged by the thimble beside it. This is a copy from Victorian stages sold for the enjoyment of children. (*Photograph by Elinor Coyle*)

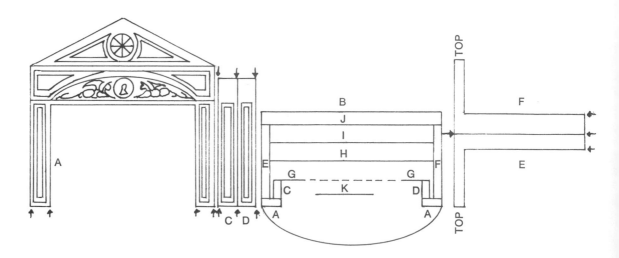

J represents another section of the mouth of the cave and the outside world. The water, bottom right, should be pale green, the rocks beside it pink with pale green shrubbery, the surrounding rock slate grey. Outside, the trees are green, the nearer land pale green, the distant mountain pink and white, the moon is left white, and the sky and water are blue.

K consists of Aladdin, a table, and the princess. Aladdin wears a red coat, green trousers and shirt, and a pale green hat. The table is red with two gold pitchers, and at the center is a blue bowl with a pineapple. The princess wears a rose-colored skirt and veil, blue bodice, and gold crown.

When dry, cut out the eleven pieces carefully. To help cut straight edges, use a metal-edged ruler as a guide. When cutting out *K*, consider it one piece and leave enough white around the group so that it can stand up. Cuts are made wherever arrows are located.

Glue *A* in place on *B* as shown. Glue the side proscenium pieces *C* and *D* onto *A* and *B*. Glue *G* onto *C*, *D*, and *B*. Glue *E* and *F* in place with the vertical "leg" at the back. Glue *H*, *I*, and *J* in their respective places to *B*, *E*, and *F*. Glue *K* in place. You may have to bend it just slightly to get it to stand up properly.

Sign your name and date on the backdrop and your Victorian toy theater is ready to entertain the children of all ages in your dollhouse. See what you can work up for other presentations.

10 Left Bank Artist's Studio

My guess is that you will have more fun assembling the artist's studio pictured here than with the previous miniature rooms, simply because it admits your using almost any furnishing in your collection.

The artist of the thirties had little money. He lived in a garret because he couldn't afford anything else. His furniture, what there was of it, was a conglomeration of oddities because he used the castoffs of everyone he knew.

The one pictured here is a duplicate of a room I actually stayed in at the end of this period. One could look out the skylight and glimpse the Grand Hotel across the Seine. Through the ceiling skylight, the indigo blue of the Paris sky was visible. Ah me, happy times!

If you will study John Blauer's artist's studio (see color plate), you will see that our minds ran in similar directions but at different levels. You will note that he used the same slanting skylight that I used (this is almost universally a part of the architecture of Paris), but he chose to look into the sky, whereas I chose to look across the river. You can make your own choice. His way is easier.

For his background behind the skylight, he had only to paint his sky. But I wanted to look out on buildings and see a huge blowup of the hotel across the river under a romantic moonlit sky. On an 11″ back wall, I wanted to bring the skylight down to about 5¼″ from the bottom because this looked about right. You may want to find a poster or large illustration that will suit your purpose. After just a few days of wrangling with my conscience, I took the hotel photo from the wall and out of its frame. I trimmed it to fit my space—20″ × 5¾″—and glued it to the back wall flush with the top.

You might use a scene of a meadow, or a street scene that gives the feeling of looking down, perhaps just the tops of trees with the sky

This Left Bank Artist's Studio of the 1930s was made by the author as a remembrance of an actual apartment. The back scene, an enlarged photo of the Grand Hotel in Paris, is viewed through a typically French skylight.

behind them. It is fun deciding on what to use. Glue your background to the back wall (or paint the back wall) very carefully.

Now go back to our original law of doing the floor first. Almost anything can be used on an attic floor—raw (unfinished) boards, old linoleum over the wood base, that sort of thing—but I used the Wallcork flooring described in Chapter 16, page 197. Notice that I dropped a few blobs of paint of different colors on the floor to add a degree of authenticity (artists are generally considered pretty sloppy) and a note of color to a room that doesn't have much brightness.

Notice that the door frame is left unfinished. The end walls are then finished with brick wallpaper.

Since there is little furniture in the studio on which to place things, I planned the shelf at back; a ⅛″ pine board 1″ wide, laid across the wall at the 5¼″ level to support the skylight. This, in turn, is supported by pilasters also cut from ⅛″ wood 1″ wide, according to the pattern given in figure 27. The back wall of the garret is then finished by gluing boards of ⅛″ wood cut 5¼″ long against the back of the box. I used Constantine's veneer glue for this and found it extraordinarily efficient. Atop these, glue the 1″ shelf to fit snugly between the two end walls. When dry, glue in the pilasters. Let dry, and then finish with one coat of clear varnish just to bring out the grain in the wood. We don't want it to look finished. Stain and sand a tiny piece of molding (not more than ⅛″ or 3⁄16″) and glue across the top of the shelf at the back edge. This will support the skylight; leave about 1⁄16″ space between the molding and the back of the box. Sand and stain a 20″ strip of ¼″ molding and glue to the ceiling 4″ from the back of the box.

Now we must go back to the basic box. Because the back supports the skylight, it must be fastened securely; glue and tack before doing the finishing outlined above. But the lid must also be fastened securely because it, too, supports the skylight. I cut the lid horizontally 4″ from the back edge and fastened the back half with glue and nails. Two ½″-square beams, unstained and unfinished, were glued to this half of the ceiling before attaching it to the box.

From the front part of the ceiling, which is 6″ wide, I cut a piece that measured 4″ deep and 8″ long. This becomes a ceiling skylight.

There is a thwarted desire of mine that you might consider for your own box. I originally cut this square to be used as an opening onto the roof of the box or building. I was going to construct a railing around it as a "widow's walk" with a stairway going up to it from the studio below. However, even in my 20″ box there wasn't room for a stairway and all I thought should go into the box, so this idea was discarded. But a builder never gives up. The opening became a skylight, and the light for the studio beams down through it from a box atop the lid.

The front half of the lid is hinged onto the back half so that it may be lifted to enable you to work inside the box. On the back half of the lid, the transformer or batteries are fastened, and tiny grooves routed out so that wires for the inside lighting may be run down through the roof. A small box to cover the transformer was then constructed, painted to match the rest of the outside of the box, and mounted over the top-side electrical work.

I tried and discarded the idea of glass for the skylights after two pieces broke. A material that works perfectly is SIG heat-forming clear plastic, which the label suggests for making canopies and bubbles. It comes in sheets, .030 × 8½″ × 17″, at one dollar per package of two sheets.

For the back skylight, you will need only about 7″. The measurement depends upon where you have installed the shelf, so measure carefully. To make the 17″ length fit my box, I simply glued a 1½″ piece to each end of the plastic using Crafty glue, and the photo demonstrates how effective this is. Strips of stained ¼″ molding were then glued, equally spaced, on the inside of the plastic. Dry under weights to prevent warping. When this is all ready, it is a simple matter to slip the plastic into the tiny groove between the molding and the shelf and brace it behind the molding you've glued on the outside edge of the top roof piece. Notice that John Blauer has used square panes in his skylight, while I have used straight pieces. Both are authentic.

For the ceiling skylight, measure the opening and cut the plastic to fit exactly. Cut ¼″ molding, stained, to fit the four sides and glue on the inside of the opening with about ⅟₁₆″ protruding over the opening. Turn this piece of the ceiling over. Glue pieces of the ¼″ molding onto the plastic and dry under weights. Make sure you cut the molding ⅛″ short to allow the plastic to come down over the inner molding at the edge. Drop the plastic in from the top; you may have to trim the molding pieces a bit to make them fit. Cut ¼″ molding to fit the outside of the opening and glue at the edge, protruding ⅟₁₆″ into the opening so as to hold the plastic. Hold with your fingers until set. Attach this front half of the box lid to the back half with 1″ hinges and tiny nails.

In-a-Door Bed

A piece I've never seen duplicated anywhere is the 1930s In-a-Door bed, which stands against the left wall of the studio. (After all, an artist has to sleep somewhere, doesn't he?) It was designed by Joen Ellen Kanze of North White Plains, New York. I have since made this piece in many versions and have always been pleased with it. It won second prize in the 1975 Originality Contest of the *Dollhouse and Miniature News*.

1 length ⅛″ cherry, basswood, or another suitable wood about 6″ square
1 length scrap wood ³⁄₁₆″ × ³⁄₁₆″ × 4″ long
3 swab sticks or ⅛″ square sticks cut 3½″ long
1 ⅛″ dowel 4½″ long to be used for hinge
  Drill for ⅛″ holes
  Stain and finish of your choice
  Small mirror and brass findings for front
  Handle for center front
  Any quick, permanent, clear glue

Using ⅛″ wood, construct a box 7″ high, 4″ wide, and deep enough to accommodate the bedstead and mattress. Drill a hole in each side about ½″ from the bottom of the box. These holes are for a 4½″ dowel that will act as a hinge for the bedstead.

Cut and finish a ½″ piece of matching wood to fit the space beneath the bedstead. Sand and finish all pieces before assembling, then glue the ½″ piece in under the bedstead openings.

Now build the bedstead. All pieces, as usual, should be sanded and finished before working with them. *A* is the end support, *B* are the dowels (cut three) used for bedstead support. Swab sticks are fine for this.

In-a-Door bed by Joen Ellen Kanze is a beautiful piece, appropriate for a studio because of the crowded space.

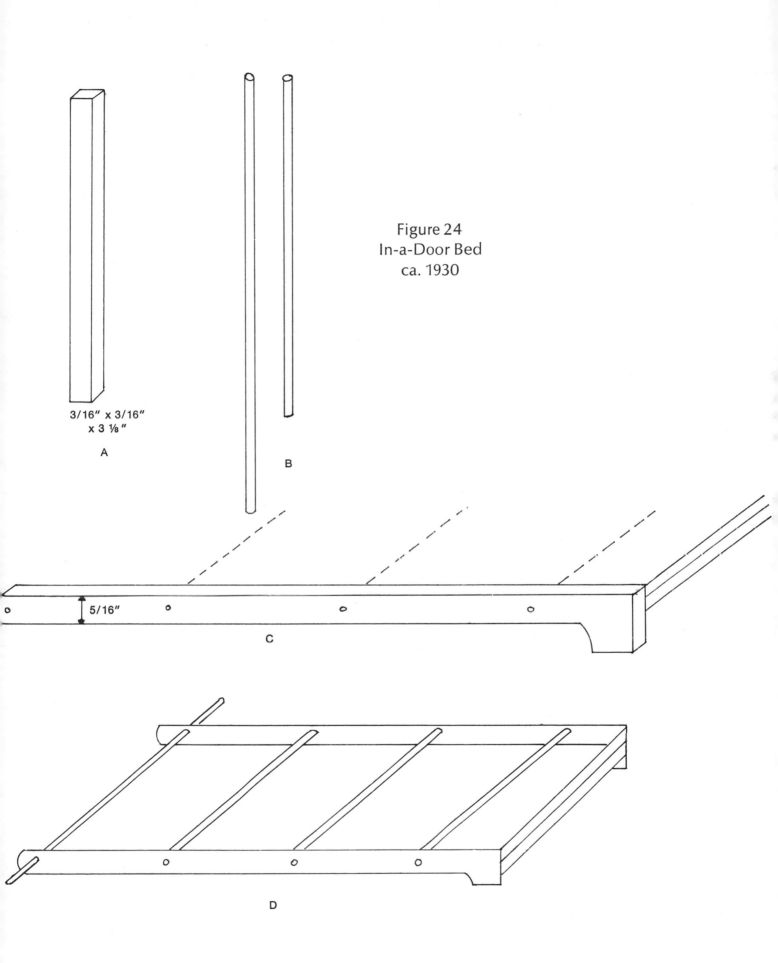

Figure 24
In-a-Door Bed
ca. 1930

3/16″ x 3/16″
x 3 ⅛ ″

A

B

5/16″

C

D

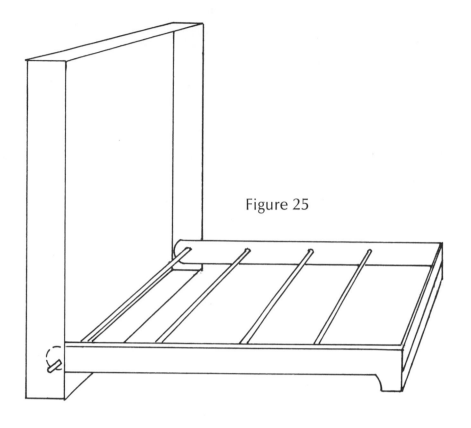

Figure 25

Cut two of *C*, ⅛″ wood cut ⁵⁄₁₆″ wide at the sides, with legs shaped at the ends. Drill ⅛″ holes at the left end for the hinge. Drill ⅛″ holes as shown for the bedstead supports. *D* shows the detail of the bedstead with the 4½″ dowel, which is to be the hinge, inserted. Apply glue to the three ⅛″ dowels before and after inserting them in the holes. Glue *A* to the side pieces (as shown in *D*) for end support. Place the hinge dowel through the bedstead from the left side to the right but *do not* glue this piece. Glue *only* at the box holes. Trim off any excess on the outside. The bedstead should now move up and down inside the box; you may have to trim a bit here and there to make the outside even.

Sand and finish the front (the ½″ piece glued beneath the bedstead) and trim with a small mirror and brass decorations, as shown in the photograph, or whatever strikes your fancy. Apply a pull down handle at center front.

MATTRESS AND PILLOW

Materials Needed for This Project
1 length narrow-stripe ticking fabric, about ¼ yard
1 length string, 44″ long
   Matching thread
   Six-strand embroidery thread
   Stuffing

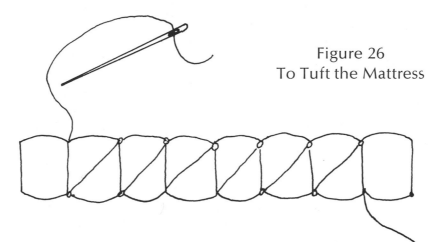

Figure 26
To Tuft the Mattress

Use ¼″ seams on both mattress and pillow. Cut two pieces of the ticking, each 6½″ × 3½″, for top and bottom. Cut two pieces each 22″ × 1″ for welting. Cut one piece 22″ × 1½″ for the sides. Cut two pieces of string, each 22″ long.

Fold the welting pieces in half, lengthwise, wrong sides together. Insert the string in the pieces, and, using a zipper foot, stitch close to the string. Trim to ¼″. Stitch this welting to the top and bottom of the side section, right sides together, raw edges even. Measure the top and bottom to be certain they will fit the bed, allowing for ¼″ seams. Starting at one corner, join the side section to the top, right sides together, and stitch in a ¼″ seam, clipping the side sections at the corners. Stitch the ends of the side sections together, cutting off the excess. Stitch the bottom to the side section in the same manner, leaving one end open for stuffing. Turn, then stuff and slip-stitch closed.

Almost anything can be used for the studio-bed stuffing: old silk stockings shredded, bits of cotton; I know one collector who saves the lint from her clothes dryer to use for this purpose! Be sure that the length of your mattress will be ¼″ short of the head of the bedstead so as not to interfere with the hinge.

Lightly mark the top and bottom of the mattress for simulated buttons. Use six-strand embroidery thread, and sew as shown in the diagram in figure 26, pulling the thread tight enough to plump up the mattress.

Joen Ellen Kanze, who executed the design for the bed, uses foam plastic and cardboard to make her mattress. Cut to fit the bedstead, again leaving ¼″ space at the head of the bed so as not to interfere with the hinges. Cover the foam with plastic and glue underneath. Cover the cardboard and glue in a similar fashion; then place the wrong side of the foam and the wrong side of the cardboard together and glue. Quilt with the Dennison Buttoneer or with a Picas button fastener, available at Woolworth stores.

For the pillow, simply cut material to fit, but twice as long as the pillow is wide. Stitch on two sides; then turn, press, and stuff. Slip-stitch the open side together.

Bead Coatrack

That handsome coatrack that in our photo is carrying the model's dress is a bead concoction created by Irene Kessler of St. Louis for the Second Annual Originality Contest staged by the *Dollhouse and Miniature News.* It is extraordinarily handsome, ranking with some of the better-made ones on the market.

Materials Needed for This Project

1 length ⅛″ metal rod, 5¼″ long, from an HO railroad shop
  Pipe cleaner
  Assorted wooden beads
  Wooden shapes for base
  Glue
  Paint

The wooden shapes were found by Ms. Kessler in a bag of such things brought from the Pink Sleigh (see Appendix). Because the beads are made of wood, the rack is very light and tends to fall over easily. I glued a lead weight the size of a quarter to the underside of the bottom wood piece to add stability. Sheet lead from the plumber, cut to shape, will accomplish the same thing.

The metal rod comes in 36″ lengths, so cut off a piece 5¼″ in length with the wire snips. Thread onto the base after gluing the two base pieces together and boring a ⅛″ hole through both. Drop a bit of glue into the hole, then insert the pipe.

String any attractive combination of wooden beads up to ¾″ from the top, adding a bit of glue with each bead. Cut the pipe cleaner in half and twist the two pieces around the rod at this point to form the four arms. Drop in a dab of glue to hold securely. Finish off with a ½″ bead and a smaller bead on the very top. Drop a dab of glue into the top bead hole and let dry. When dry, snip off the metal rod so that it's even with the top bead.

Slip one long bead and one small bead on each of the pipe cleaner arms; trim the pipe cleaner to the proper length, leaving about ⅛″ to fold over, and twist to hold the beads. Bend up the little beads on the end; these are to hold the hats.

Figure 27

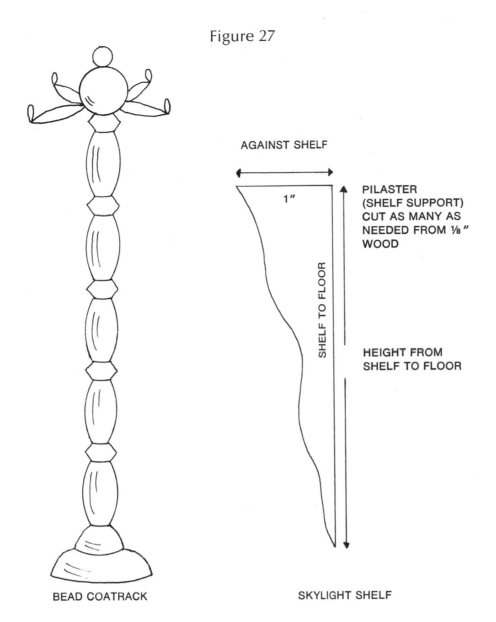

AGAINST SHELF

1"

SHELF TO FLOOR

PILASTER
(SHELF SUPPORT)
CUT AS MANY AS
NEEDED FROM ⅛"
WOOD

HEIGHT FROM
SHELF TO FLOOR

BEAD COATRACK

SKYLIGHT SHELF

Paint the rack brown or black and the top bead and small ones on the arms gold.

Ms. Kessler's original entry was left a flat, matte black; however, it is very handsome painted with acrylic paint and then top-coated with decoupage glaze.

Artist's Palette and Brushes

We show a pattern for three sizes of a palette here, so you may trace the one that is best in scale with your doll. The largest may be cut from ⅛" pine or basswood; you will then have no trouble in boring the ⅛" hole where the artist's thumb is inserted. The second size may be

Figure 28
Artist's Palette

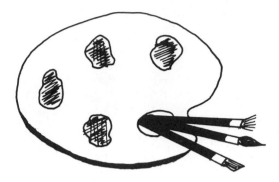

CUT FROM ⅛"
PINE OR BASSWOOD

CUT FROM ⅛"
MAT BOARD

CUT FROM ⅛"
BALSA OR CARDBOARD

cut from balsa wood, but it has a tendency to split when you bore the thumbhold; basswood or mat board seems to work better. The smallest size is very successful merely cut from cardboard. The hole is then cut with a nail scissors. Drop a little mound of color in five or six places on the board.

Make a few brushes by sanding or whittling 1" pieces of 1/16"-square strips to a round and to a point at the bottom. Cut a few strands of hair from an old wig or off the bottom of your own hair. Cut a tiny strip of heavyweight aluminum foil ⅛" wide and about 1" long. Lay this on the workboard. Lay the hair on it with the bottom ends matching and the top of the hair sticking out about ⅛". Gently fold the foil over and over, then crimp in place with your pliers or glue with Krazy glue.

11 Art Deco Clubroom

"Anything goes" was the catch phrase for the 1920s, and it captures the spirit of Art Deco that is exemplified in this room. And anything goes when you're planning the decorating of such a miniature, for it was a period of exploration, a wild effort to shake off the effects of one war at the same time we were speeding towards another.

If you plan your miniature rooms to capture certain moments in time, this is a fitting subject, for there was a most charming and humorous side to it, and the interior decoration and design was unlike anything we'd seen before or will ever see again most likely.

You'll find a world of inspiration for the planning of such a room, for there were a number of great exhibitions dedicated to it, and several books have been written about it. They all bring back memories of flappers with chests like men (accomplished by tying folded dinner napkins tightly around their breasts), dancing the Charleston in above-the-knee dresses, which in that era were considered very daring at the cocktail parties and *thés dansants* that were all the rage.

In interior decorating, Art Deco meant total design. I tried three wallpapers before I happened upon the piece of silk that you see on the walls of my clubroom. None quite exemplified the period, but when I found this silk with its ziggurats of white, blue, tan, and black, I knew that it was perfect for the straight lines of lucite, steel, and walnut that would have been found in one of the gentleman's clubs of the day.

Madeline Gesser, an interior designer of Hewlett Harbor, New York, makes and markets this miniature furniture. It calls for a great deal of expertise if you are going to try to make it yourself. I'm going to give you directions for the two club chairs, but the really great ideas here are in the architecture of the room itself.

Since I had already applied two coats of wallpaper when I found the silk (it was a housecoat from the 1950s found at a rummage sale), I

Clubroom in the Art Deco style has a false wall at rear covered with an Art Deco silk, while floors are made of hand-laid parquet. Notice the little radio at the rear on the bar. Contemporary furniture by Madeline Gesser.

Silk wall covering, chosen after the butterfly paper shown on the walls seemed too "tame," is mounted on poster board. The wall is completed with cornice and baseboard and then slipped into place over the back wall. (*Photograph by Elinor Coyle*)

used false walls, which have since been used again and again in building miniature rooms. They are particularly valuable since the paper or fabric that is to cover the walls is mounted on poster board (shirt board is not quite heavy enough for this job) and glued.

First, cut the poster board by placing it against the outside walls of the room and carefully marking the dimensions and location of the openings. They must be exact. Cut out doors and windows carefully. Now place the poster board against the inside of the walls and check to make sure that windows and doors on the board correspond exactly with those on the walls. Do this for all three walls.

To cover these false walls, cut a piece of fabric or paper about 2″ larger than the poster board on all sides. Place the board in the center and fold the excess material to the back and glue all around. Allow to dry thoroughly.

When dry, make cuts in the openings from center to corners. Fold the material to the back and glue, stretching tightly but not so tightly that the poster board becomes bent. If you are covering with paper, this is no problem at all, but if you are using a thin piece of silk, as I was, great care must be taken to make sure that the design of the fabric is not stretched out of shape. Let the pieces dry under a weight to prevent any warping. Door frames and window frames are now glued in place on the false walls; then the whole thing is slipped into the shell of the room. If you have been careful, it should fit perfectly.

This is a great technique if you are using fabric that might become spotted if applied directly to glue. It is also most valuable because if you should decide to use the box shell for something else, you have only to pull out the walls and prepare other walls for the new undertaking.

You will notice that we have used no door or window frames in this particular room. This was the period in which door and window openings began to appear with no frames around them, probably an extension of the Art Deco preoccupation with simple lines. The plain slab door soon appeared, also, and is still seen today—not for art's sake as it was in the 1930s, but because it is less expensive. We felt that because the design in our wall covering was so very strong, frames would only detract from it. For the same reason, baseboards, ceiling cornices, and picture frames in this room were painted flat black to pick up the black in the wall covering—a most interesting and amusing idea, typical of the startling things done in this period.

Parquet Floors

Typical of the fun you'll have in doing a room in the Art Deco style was my quest for a floor covering. Carpets and wall-to-wall coverings just didn't seem right. Bare floors belonged to another period. I settled on parquet floors.

There are a number of designs that you might work on if you decide to make a parquet floor; some of them are shown. I decided that plain squares (A) of 1″ (1′ in people size) would be best with our furniture.

Constantine's $\frac{1}{28}$″ veneer woods are perfect and are easily cut with either the X-acto No. 1 knife or your scissors; the only thing necessary is to be exact in your measurements so the pieces will fit together when combined. Try for a light wood and a dark wood so you have contrast, as I have in this floor. Here, I might recommend Constantine's Introductory Veneering Kit, which for around five dollars provides everything you need for this job: a pint of special veneer glue; two square feet each of teak, walnut, mahogany, and primavera from Mexico; and a complete set of instructions.

Cut all the pieces needed at once; when the glue is on the floor, it won't wait while you cut more pieces. For a box of the size I use (20″ × 11″), you will need 240 1″ pieces, or 120 of each color. Mark three or four lines on the floor base with a pencil, from one side to the other, to guide you in placing the squares. Start at the front, in the center. Spread a thin coating of the glue over about 3″ of floor, the entire width of the floor. Starting at the center mark, lay the squares in alternating color. For additional contrast in this floor, I also alternated the grain of the veneer; dark squares were laid with the grain up and down, light squares with the grain from right to left.

Remember that this special veneer glue needs only a thin spread to hold the veneer. If the glue is so thick that it comes up between the squares, then you'll be in trouble, for it dries too fast to get it up. Working quickly, lay the first three rows, then apply the glue and lay the squares for the next three rows. Check with the penciled lines as you go along to be certain that the squares are straight. You will have to trim the end squares a bit to fit the box; measure and trim before applying.

When the entire floor is in place, rub well with your palm, then dry under a weight to prevent warping. The squares may also be laid corner to corner and are very effective in this pattern, but this will necessitate cutting the end squares in half diagonally at the ends of the rows.

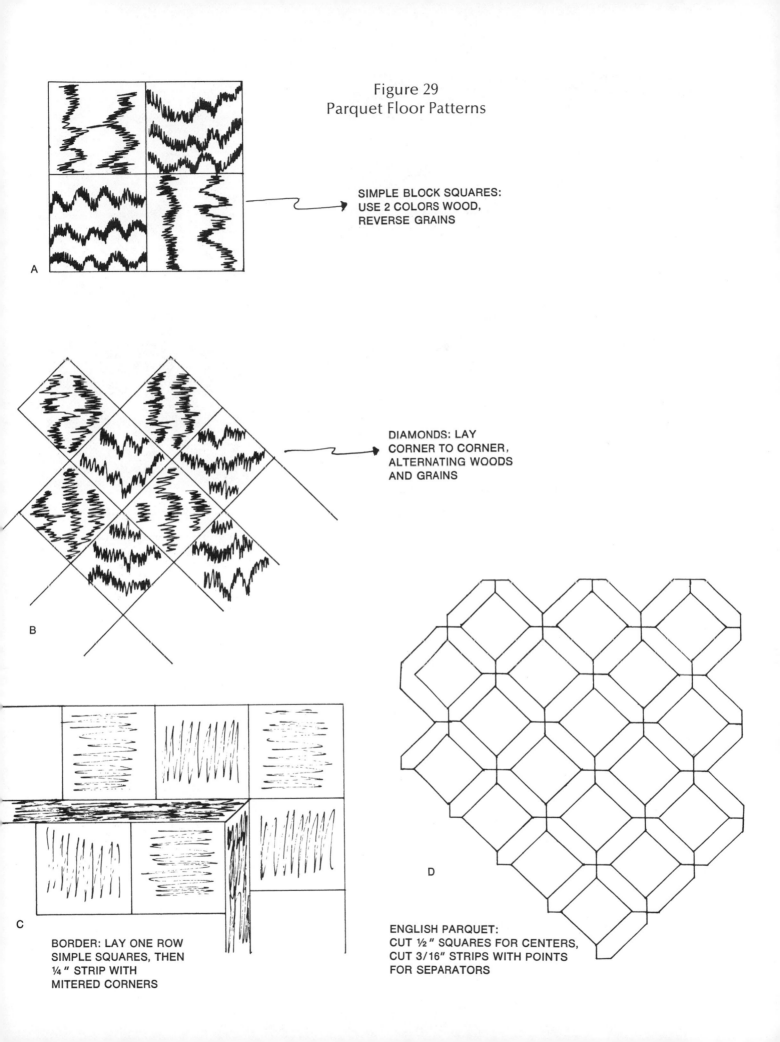

Figure 29
Parquet Floor Patterns

SIMPLE BLOCK SQUARES:
USE 2 COLORS WOOD,
REVERSE GRAINS

DIAMONDS: LAY
CORNER TO CORNER,
ALTERNATING WOODS
AND GRAINS

BORDER: LAY ONE ROW
SIMPLE SQUARES, THEN
¼ " STRIP WITH
MITERED CORNERS

ENGLISH PARQUET:
CUT ½ " SQUARES FOR CENTERS,
CUT 3/16" STRIPS WITH POINTS
FOR SEPARATORS

A

B

C

D

Posters were the great fad of this period. These two miniposters, lithographed on card, were found in the sale of a private collection. (*Photograph by Elinor Coyle*)

Dry for at least four or five hours, preferably overnight, then either wax or finish with two or three coats of decoupage glaze. I like this best since it seems to deepen the color of the woods a bit.

The chandelier was made especially for this clubroom by a friend of the author, copied from one designed by René Lalique in 1932 for the steamer *Normandie*. The posters, which serve as the only wall decorations, were cut from an art catalogue for an Art Deco show recently held in New York. Posters were very important in this period. The 1924 *Studio* (special poster number) concludes: "Poster designers are producing some of the most outstanding work of our time." Watch for reproductions in the proper scale in magazines and book advertisements.

The cocktail shaker and glasses were especially made for the author by Kendall Ewer of Colonial Craftsmen, but we have heard from many readers of *Dollhouse and Miniature News* that they have picked up a few miniature shakers at antique sales and shops that were produced in the 1920s as toothpick holders, canapé-stick holders, and other amusing concepts. Keep your eyes open and you may come across a treasure on your next shopping or "just looking" trip.

Notice, too, that I have used two Queen Anne chairs in this room, mainly to provide interest and prevent the blatant modernism from becoming too overpowering. This is a decorating trick used by many interior designers, and a most welcome one with miniaturists who may have some extra chairs from another period that must be used!

Veneered Walls

It was obvious from the beginning that with a room such as this, where it seemed necessary to use some of the designs of the period to establish a mood, it would be necessary to use them on the walls but to keep some portion of the walls plain and unpatterned, since most of the designs of the period were so extravagant. I decided upon veneering the two end walls, with the design on the back as it appears in the photo.

We've discussed veneering rather generally in directions for the floor in the Federal music room (see page 62) and for the parquet floor in this room, but veneering of walls is a different story.

You must have two tools: a sharp knife and a veneer roller. Don't let anyone tell you that you must buy a veneer roller; the brayer that you use for wallpapering will do nicely for the veneer. You will have numerous sources for the knife, of course, but Constantine's offers a veneer saw that costs only about two dollars and does beautiful work. The saw is guided by a straightedge and makes clean cuts so that perfect fitting joints are assured.

When using veneers of $\frac{1}{28}''$ thickness, I find that a pair of scissors sometimes does satisfactory work; although if the veneer is very dry and "crisp," it sometimes splits when the scissors blade is inserted.

Your very best bet, if you are a beginner with veneers, is the Introductory Veneering Kit discussed on page 132. The panels shown in the photo of the clubroom are the most simple you can make. Select a very thin narrow molding, in this case $\frac{1}{8}''$ wide and $\frac{1}{16}''$ thick. Stain and let dry. Do all of your cutting and fitting on the veneer before it is attached to the wall. Measure and mark the place in which the panels will go. Cut the molding using mitered corners. Stain and varnish the veneer. Turn your box on end so that the wall you are working on is on the worktable. Spread a thin, even coat of the veneer glue over the veneer. Fit onto the wall, press carefully, and then roll the veneer carefully so

This wing back fireplace made by Wesley Faurot illustrates how the buildup of molding and paneling gives depth and richness to paneled walls.

that it is completely flat, with no bulges. Dry under pressure, but go back every thirty minutes or so and roll it again so that there can be no air trapped against the wall.

Now, attach the molding and dry under pressure. Use only ordinary white glue to attach the molding; veneer glue sets too quickly and won't allow you to maneuver the corners into place.

I am reprinting here the Wesley Faurot's corner "wing back" paneled fireplace from *The Collector's Guide to Dollhouses and Dollhouse Miniatures*. Notice that this is still a simple panel, using only the beauty of the wood for decoration, but it is very effective. Here the veneer is attached, then a panel of $\frac{1}{16}''$ wood is cut slightly smaller and beveled on all sides. This is then glued to the base. The same procedure is used in the narrow panels at the side of the fireplace. Notice, too, that the molding at the edge of the panel is carried all the way to the floor. The bottom of the center panel, over the fireplace, is then outlined with the molding, making a butt joint.

You will experience enormous satisfaction in working with veneers. In the little panels you have outlined with molding, for example, you might attach any of the small carved designs that are offered in many catalogues. Notice that in this room I have used on one wall a Victorian clock from Miniature Mart (see Appendix) for an opulent effect. A poster is used on the opposite panel.

You will find many directions for the final finish of your paneled rooms. I have come to prefer decoupage lacquer, satin finish rather than gloss, to any other. One, produced by the Houston Art and Frame Company of Houston, Texas, dries to the touch in fifteen minutes and is used after a sealer has been applied to the veneer. While this dries very quickly and the makers say it can be sanded and recoated within one hour, you'd be wise to let the first coats dry overnight so there's no danger of the finish "balling." Apply about five coats and sand between each coat with No. 400 wet sandpaper (the sandpaper must be used wet). To attain a rubbed finish, use fine steel wool (4/0 grit) after the final coat, then wax.

Club Chair

Our club chair made by Madeline Gesser is typical of club chairs found all over the world during the 1930s and is so handsome that it deserves a room of its own. It is extraordinarily simple to make since it is all angles and straight lines. Sides and back are cut from ½" wood, mahogany or walnut, and the seat is cut from ¾" wood. All pieces are carefully sanded and finished before the chair is put together. Notice that the back edges of the arms are mitered, as are the sides of the back piece. These are glued together, then the seat is fitted into them, all even at the bottom, and glued.

Materials Needed for This Project
1 length walnut or mahogany, ½" thick and about 8" long
1 length walnut or mahogany, ¾" thick and about 2" long
1 length fine black leather, 1½" wide and about 8" long
1 piece small stainless steel or silvered lead or wood square 1½" × 1½" for base
Glue

Above requirements are for one chair. To make a sofa, enlarge seat and back twice (for a two-seater) or three times (for a three-seater) and proceed as directed. Enlarge cushion measurements in the same proportion.

Mrs. Gesser uses fine black glove leather for the upholstery. Fold

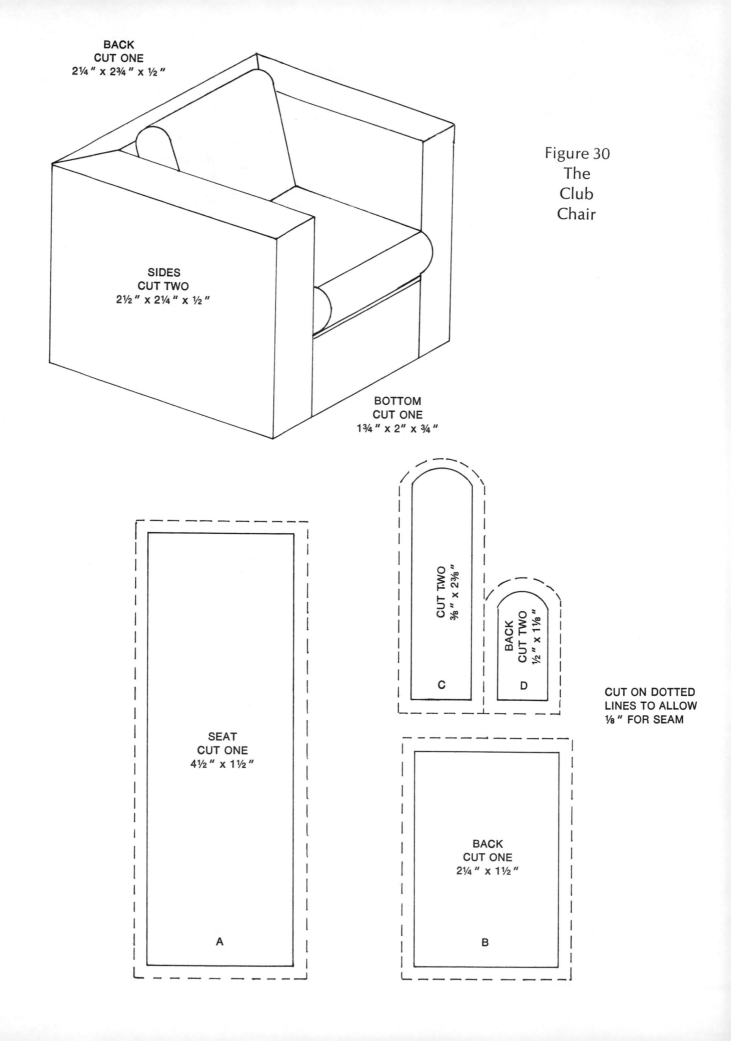

BACK
CUT ONE
2¼ " x 2¾ " x ½ "

Figure 30
The
Club
Chair

SIDES
CUT TWO
2½ " x 2¼ " x ½ "

BOTTOM
CUT ONE
1¾ " x 2" x ¾ "

CUT TWO
⅜ " x 2⅜ "

C

BACK
CUT TWO
½ " x 1⅛ "

D

CUT ON DOTTED
LINES TO ALLOW
⅛ " FOR SEAM

SEAT
CUT ONE
4½ " x 1½ "

A

BACK
CUT ONE
2¼ " x 1½ "

B

Contemporary chairs and table by Madeline Gesser are made of solid walnut and steel with leather upholstery. Table top is of ¼" Plexiglass.

the seat, piece *A*, in half. Fit the gusset, piece *C*, between the side edges to be sure it fits; then stitch on the two sides, stuff with a little cotton, and stitch shut along the back edge. Do the same with the back, piece *B*, and its gussets, which are piece *D*. These should fit into the chair nicely, the back resting upon the seat. Glue. Mrs. Gesser uses a piece of heavy stainless steel, 1½" square by ¼" thick, glued in the center of the bottom of the chair for looks (otherwise the chair seems to hug the floor too closely), as counterpoint to the dark wood, and to furnish stability.

Atwater Kent Cathedral Radio

No well-outfitted living room in the 1930s was without a little table-model radio; the Atwater Kent Cathedral Radio, so-called because it was said to resemble a cathedral window, was the most popular. One can be made from a scrap of ¾" wood, properly stained and finished, but I much prefer making it on a core of ¾" balsa, veneered.

Materials Needed for This Project
1 piece ¹⁄₁₆" wood for base (figure 31, *B*)
1 piece ¾" balsa or other wood, 2" long
1 piece scrap veneer, about 2" wide and 6" long
　Very fine sandpaper
　Stain and finishing lacquer
　Black-headed pins
1 scrap of gold foil
　Glue

Figure 31
Atwater Kent Cathedral Radio
ca. 1930

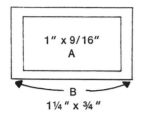

1" x 9/16"
A

B
1¼" x ¾"

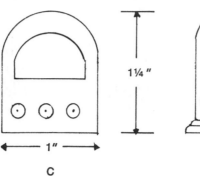

1¼"

1"

C

D

Stock veneer, ⅟₂₈″ thick, does very nicely for this piece. Cut the core of balsa according to figure 31, C ¾″ thick. Round off the top according to the pattern; sand carefully so the round is smooth and even. You will need a piece of the veneer about 2″ wide and 6″ long. Place this to soak in warm water in a deep plate while you are working on the core. Test it after about ten minutes; it should be easily bendable. Cut a strip ¾″ wide and long enough to go around the core on two sides and the top. Spread this part of the core thinly with glue, then gently shape the veneer strip around it. Fasten by wrapping with a rubber band. The bottom of the veneer must come exactly to the bottom of the core.

Now cut two pieces of the veneer for the front and back. (I like to use veneer slightly moistened for cutting; it is much easier to handle.) Glue one piece to the back of the core, making certain that you have a clean seam between the side and the back. Dry under pressure.

While this is drying, cut out the space for the speaker grille in the front piece of veneer, using the No. 2 X-acto knife. One cover for the grille that is tremendously effective is a small piece of curtain mesh in very fine squares, painted gold. This glues directly against the balsa core. Another effective grille is made by staining the balsa core brown in the space where the grille will go and then gluing against it a ½″ bell cap that has been pressed out flat and the bottom wings cut off. Whatever you use, it must be cut to exactly fit the space cut into the front veneer piece, since the veneer must fit over it and flush against the balsa. Glue this into place.

A nice finish for the bottom is to glue the two pieces *A* and *B* together with the back edges flush. Stain and finish; then glue the finished balsa core on top, back edges flush.

A tiny nameplate may be cut from gold foil for just beneath the grille in the front. The dials are heavy drawing paper cut into the smallest possible circles, with stations marked on the circles with black ink. For the knobs, cut black-headed map pins to about ½″ long and stick in through the center.

You can almost hear the music coming out!

Beaded Portieres

I worked a long time on the beaded portieres shown in this room. You can make them of beads, but somehow they don't look like beaded portieres to someone who actually *knew* beaded portieres. The ones that finally won a place in the clubroom were masculine, I thought, elegant, and practical. All you will need is some ⅛″ brass tubing, six-strand embroidery floss, and the necessary beads.

I ran into the same problem encountered in hanging the door curtain in the Victorian theater; I was unable to formulate a holder for the rod that would be small enough to fit against the ⅜″ door frame of the plywood. The entire frame was finally lined with strips of 1/16″ basswood, ⅜″ wide, top and sides, and a threshold was glued against the floor. Quarter-inch cup hooks were used as the hangers; these were screwed into the top of the door frame about ¼″ from the sides. After these are installed, try fitting your brass rod into them to make certain that it will fit.

Perhaps you will remember that some beaded portieres were made of glass beads strung on chain. The ones I reproduce were made of wooden beads strung on cord. Measurements here, again, will vary with the height of your door and the tightness of your knots, but for a 7″ door I cut lengths of the six-strand embroidery floss 17½″ long for the longest, next to the frame, 16″ for the next, 14″ for the next, and 12″ for the shortest.

If you are using wooden beads (which I prefer), try to select some intriguing shapes. The diamond-shaped ones shown in our drawing are from Westrim Novelties, their No. 2830, and come twenty-four to the package. You will need three packages for each door. Those painted black seem to be finished in some sort of quantity operation, and you will need to push a pin, or the end of a paper clip, through each one to remove excess paint.

Starting with the shortest one, string a bead on each end, push it up

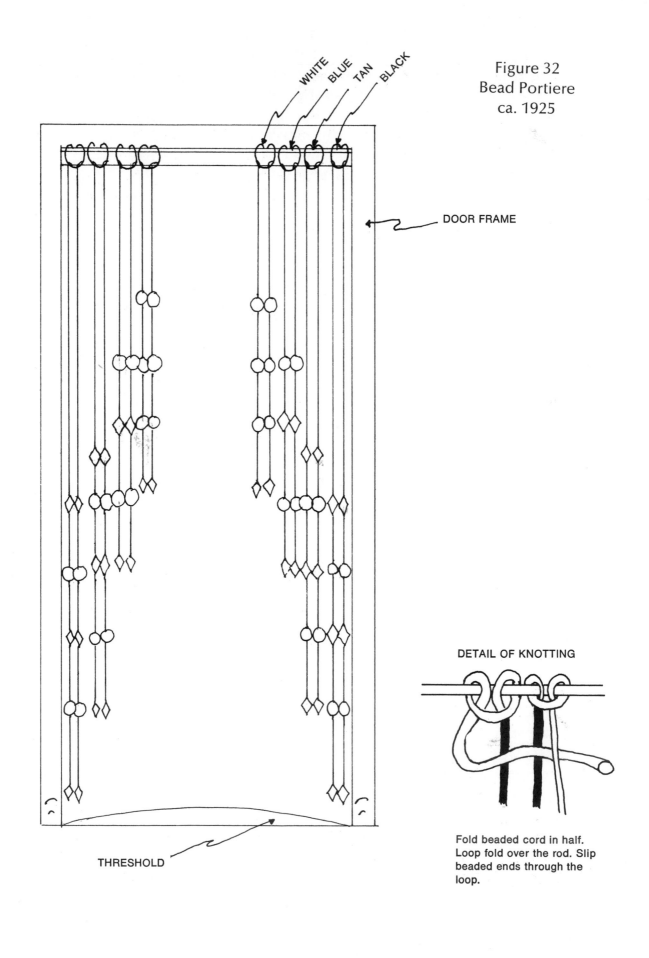

WHITE BLUE TAN BLACK

Figure 32
Bead Portiere
ca. 1925

DOOR FRAME

DETAIL OF KNOTTING

Fold beaded cord in half.
Loop fold over the rod. Slip
beaded ends through the
loop.

THRESHOLD

about 3" from the end, and tie a knot to hold it. String another bead, tie another knot about 1" down, and repeat until you come to the bottom. Then string a bead on each end and tie a knot. It should be a double knot on the ends. This is where you may go astray on measurements. If you tie loose knots, a single knot will take up about ¼" of the thread. If you tie tight knots, it will take much less. Thus, you will find it best to work with one strand of thread until you find the lengths are working out right—the strand closest to the frame reaching the floor, and the others shortening, as shown in figure 32.

Now, fold the beaded thread in half. Pull the loop over the curtain rod. Pull the ends of the thread through the loop so the thread comes to the front. Pull tight. Use colors of thread to harmonize with your room decoration. If you are making a Victorian room and want to include one of those storied "Turkish corners," it should be beaded all around.

When your rod is completely strung, slip it into the cup hooks at the top of the door. It should have been cut close enough so that it fits very snugly into the door frame.

12 Corner Drugstore, ca.1930

Since there is great pleasure in reproducing in miniature a scene that holds fond memories, I often wonder why more miniaturists do not attempt to recreate drugstores. Apothecary shops, of course, are made by the dozen, but they are necessarily small and without much detail because that's the way that apothecary shops *were*. The drugstore, however, requires a mass of detail just as the country store does, so it has infinite possibilities.

During the 1930s, most drugstores, like saloons, were located on corners for easy access. To reproduce this one properly, you will have to make a corner on your box. At either back corner measure about 3½″ back on the side and the back. This will give you a 5¼″ diagonal for the entrance. Leave the roof and floor intact; simply cut off the sides at the 3½″ point. I inlaid bricks on this corner, since that was what was generally used as an entrance floor. Cover the ceiling of this entrance corner with veneer wood or wood-printed paper. The post at the point of the roof (the corner) is most important. Although in the photo of my corner drugstore it doesn't show up too well, I varnished this copiously; when the box is viewed from the front, the corner definitely establishes itself as the crux of the whole design. Most such posts seemed to be of about 12″ diameter, so I looked for a 1″ diameter dowel. They are not readily available. However, a mop stick is exactly 1″ in diameter, so I simply sawed off the rounded end of the mop stick and cut off my post to fit my box. (You'll find that you can still use the mop, even though the shortened stick makes it necessary for you to bend over a bit as you do the daily chores.)

Shorten your post so that you can use a ⅛″ base and finial for the post. Cut these about 1½″ square and round off the edges a bit. A great deal is added by routing out a few ridges along the sides. Glue the base to the corner at the bottom of the box and then glue the post (after

Corner drugstore of the 1930s was made by the author. Note the ceiling fan by Amity Petite and the graffiti around the telephone. To carry out the idea of the corner store, the right corner of the box was actually cut off. The *Post*, found in every corner store, was meticulously reproduced.

finishing) against it. Top the post with the second base and glue again. Close the lid against the glued post and bases and allow to dry. This will hold very nicely when the lid is lifted, but it will not endure rough treatment.

The only remaining problem is building the angled wall between the side walls and over the corner entrance. Many stores used a glass transom here with the street number etched on it. I preferred Lou Kummerow's stained-glass transom (see above) in order to bring some color into the room. You will have the pieces cut from the side walls left over. I give you my measurements, but make certain that they fit your room. The angled wall above the door must fit exactly in order to support the two side walls.

Use a piece of ⅜″ plywood, 2¼″ deep and 4¾″ wide. Cut this and make sure it fits. Also cut a piece ½″ wide and 4¾″ long to form the top of the door frame. Wallpaper the top piece. Glue two pieces of ⅛″ ornamental molding on the bottom of the papered piece and insert the stained glass. On each end, fill in with pieces of any ornamental molding that will bring the stained glass to meet the side walls. On the ½″-wide piece of plywood, glue two pieces of the ⅛″ ornamental molding as

Ice-cream parlor by Iova Vaughn of the Beehive Studio is dated 1900 but seems at least 1940 by virtue of the booths and the elaborate dispensing equipment behind the soda fountain. Here, again, we find the ubiquitous rubber plant. (*Photograph by George Peterson, courtesy of the Beehive Studio*)

you did to the bottom of the papered piece. Slip this piece over the transom and the fill-in pieces, and glue. When all is dry and secure, slip this angle piece between the side walls, and glue. Secure further with small staples (No. 5 aluminum-wire cloth staples); then cut pieces of ½" stripping 1/16" thick, and glue to the sides and top to form the door frame.

Miniature Mart's flocked wallpaper was used in my room. In the second drugstore (ice-cream parlor) that is shown above, notice that the walls are whitewashed, and flocked paper is added only as a valance.

Only rarely were wood floors encountered in drugstores. I used one of Miniature Mart's elegant tile papers, which exactly resemble old-time oilcloth when varnished. In the ice-cream parlor the designer used black-and-white tiles. Either look authentic.

Because the view was outward with the door at right rear, I sawed a 4" × 6" front window in the back wall and installed a piece of heavy plexiglass, holding this to the installed frame with strips of ⅛" molding. If you want to put a name on your window (and you certainly should) and are not too proficient at lettering freehand, sheets of punch-out letters in various sizes and styles are available from stationery stores and are fun to affix. Do this lettering before the window is installed. You can draw lines on a sheet of paper and clip this to the underside of the window to guide your lettering or pasting.

The outside of this box is finished in brick-design paper, with a nice cornice in white at the top. Paint or stain might also be used. The awning, of course, is an absolute necessity.

You have, we should hope, a cache of materials you have been collecting; as every miniaturist knows, you must save everything. At least five years ago, a friend had a curtain made for an elegant bath-house, and when she showed me the material—a weatherproofed, very fine, supple canvas of green stripes on white—I begged a quarter of a yard. It proved absolutely perfect for the awning, in perfect scale. Cut a piece 6¾" long by 4" wide (the stripes going the short way); then mark and cut carefully ½" scallops on the bottom edge. No need to finish, for weatherproofed material doesn't ravel. If you are using ordinary material, however, we would advise painting the edge of the scallops carefully with white glue.

If you have tried but haven't found an appropriate awning material, simply use a very heavy white typing or drawing paper—anything with a hard finish. Cut it out as directed; then carefully draw stripes on it in any pattern you wish, and color with water color or Mongol colored pencils.

Using wire from a lightweight coat hanger (preferably white), cut two pieces 6½" long. Using a pair of ordinary pliers and the needle-nosed pliers, bend each wire to a right angle 2½" from one end. Then, 1¼" from this angle, make a second bend so that the ends meet, which will give you a diagonal about 2¾" long. Press the ends together; they don't need to be joined.

Cut a piece of the wire the length of the awning and, about ½" from the top, affix it to the material on the wrong side. Cut wire the same length and affix it to the awning at the top of the scallops, also on the wrong side. Use masking tape or Mystic tape for both these operations. Now, using Mystic tape or a tape of a color that isn't too noticeable, fold the ends of the awning over the diagonal of the wire and fasten on the right side with the tape. You will have to trim the scallop edge a bit, as this won't fold over with the rest of the edge. Now, fit the metalwork against the window opening, about ¼" above the top of the window, and fasten against the back of the box with masking tape. Fasten the vertical edge of the metal frame against the back of the box. That's all!

One must remember that one is looking out from the *inside* of the box. Be sure to mount your awning with the right side inward, so the color will show. After all, no one will see the back of your box.

Wall Shelves

I didn't make my counters; they are from Carlson's miniatures (see Appendix) and are so fine that I feel I can't equal them. If you want to try a counter, directions are provided for one later in this chapter in the material about Jean Johnson's bakery. There, the curved counter was made by Mary Kopriva.

The high shelves on the left wall, however, are a nice exercise in cabinetmaking, and you'll enjoy applying your expertise to this design.

Materials Needed for This Project
2 lengths $\frac{1}{16}''$ basswood, $3\frac{3}{16}''$ wide and $6\frac{7}{8}''$ long, *A*
2 lengths $\frac{1}{16}''$ basswood, $1\frac{3}{16}''$ wide and $6\frac{1}{4}''$ long, *B*
1 length $\frac{1}{16}''$ basswood, $2\frac{1}{4}''$ wide and $6\frac{3}{8}''$ long, *C*
4 lengths $\frac{1}{8}''$ basswood, $1\frac{1}{8}''$ wide and $1''$ long, *D*
2 lengths $\frac{1}{16}''$ basswood, $\frac{1}{2}''$ wide and $2\frac{1}{2}''$ long, *E*
1 length $\frac{1}{4}''$ corner molding, $\frac{1}{8}''$ thick and $2'$ long
1 length $\frac{1}{8}''$ ornamental molding or trim, $1\frac{1}{2}'$ long
   Stain and varnish
   Glue
8 map pins with white heads

Cut all pieces and, before doing anything, fit them all together with masking tape to make certain they fit. The width of a pencil point in your measuring can make a big difference here.

Stain and finish.

Finish the front base completely. Bevel off the edges of the door and drawer fronts with fine sandpaper, touch up a bit with stain if necessary. Glue to the base front as shown in the diagram. Snip off the stems of the map pins and push the pins into the door and drawer fronts.

Cut the corner molding to fit the base, flush with the back and with mitered corners at the front. Glue the bottom into the corner of the molding. Glue the sides into the corner molding and flush with both the front base and the back of the bottom. Allow to dry, then on the inside glue pieces of $\frac{1}{4}''$ strips to reinforce.

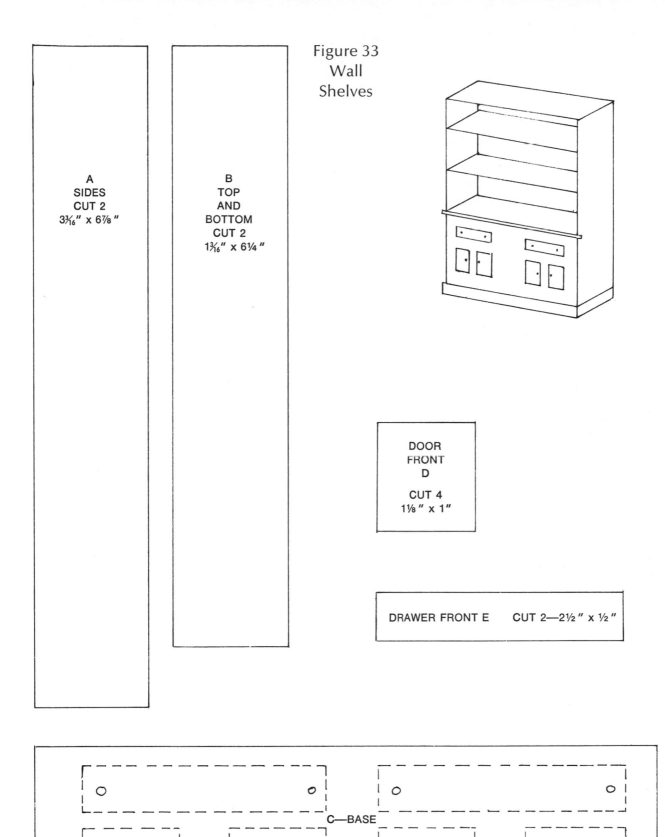

Figure 33
Wall
Shelves

A
SIDES
CUT 2
3 3/16" x 6 7/8"

B
TOP
AND
BOTTOM
CUT 2
1 3/16" x 6 1/4"

DOOR
FRONT
D

CUT 4
1 1/8" x 1"

DRAWER FRONT E   CUT 2—2 1/2" x 1/2"

C—BASE

CUT ONE
6 3/8" x 2 1/4"

Glue the top onto the top of the two sides. It should fit exactly flush. A strip of $\frac{1}{16}''$ wood serves as the top of the counter. Glue it in flush with the back, and it should project a bit at front. On the two sides and the top of the top part, glue the $\frac{1}{8}''$ ornamental molding against the front of the wood.

Cut the shelves carefully, as you did the top of the counter, so that they fit exactly between the two sides. Glue $1\frac{3}{16}''$ pieces of the $\frac{1}{8}''$ ornamental molding where you want the shelves to go. Slide the shelves in on top of these braces and glue.

Since most of the woodwork of this period was very ornamental, you could cut a piece of $1''$ commercial molding in half and glue it to the top of the shelves. Or, you might plan to cut your own molding on a jigsaw and use this.

Another Approach

While we're on the subject of stores, there are, of course, so many ideas that it would be impossible to cover them all. General stores have been made by the thousands, largely, I suspect, because it is so much fun to collect all the appurtenances that fill a general store's shelves. A tour through your catalogues will turn up enough of these items to fully equip your store. The original box may be made from the directions given in Chapter 5.

Apothecary shops have been made in great numbers, too, but since the originals were quite small, these have been mostly vignettes.

I have never seen another bakery shop such as the one pictured here, which is displayed at Jean Johnson Miniatures, Allenwood General Store, Allenwood, New Jersey. It is fascinating. The dimensions are about the same as those used in the author's boxes. This group of enthusiasts have created a most convincing scene.

The box itself, made of $\frac{3}{8}''$ plywood, is papered on the inside with wallpaper from J. Hermes (see Appendix). The Americana pattern is used in the bakery, and while wood-effect paper is usually used for floors, here it is used on the walls to simulate paneling. On the outside, it was painted with flat barn red latex paint; then bricks were drawn on with black marker pens. The entire surface was then antiqued, producing a most engaging effect that might be used on any box that houses a room with outside walls. The partition between the bakery and the kitchen is made of $\frac{1}{2}''$ plywood brought to within $6''$ of the front edge. Two slender turned legs from an old table are then glued at front and on the

Ingenious use of a large box to make two rooms—a bakery and kitchen, executed by a group for Jean Johnson Miniatures. Everything here was made by hand. Note the rubber plant at left center and the dolls dressed by Barbara Molteni. The box is 24½″ wide, 10½″ deep, and 10¾″ high. (*Photograph by Muller Studio*)

edge of the plywood to simulate an opening, giving the feeling of massive columns. Across the top of the opening, to bring it down to the dimensions of a door, is a jigsawed panel of wood in an intricate design with a fancy metal medallion in the center.

Mary Kopriva made the cabinets. The one in the rear has a large mirror from the dime store, mounted in the center. Shelves and counter are all made from lumber from Northeastern Scale Models, Inc. (see Appendix), all of which would be simple to do. The white knobs on the doors are from heads of white map pins. Paper doilies are cut apart and glued to the shelves as so many bakers use them. A careful study of the top decoration will illustrate that the wood top molding is merely a strip cut at the ends with a jigsaw. The center is a piece of gold decoupage border.

In this case, all cases and counters are made by hand, whereas those in the drugstore discussed earlier in this chapter were purchased. It is a matter of your choice, but you must work the patterns out on graph paper until you have what you want; it is impossible to decide upon patterns without knowing what dimensions you are working with.

Cut the top and bottom of the curved case at left from ⅛″ wood to the size and depth that fits your room. Sand all edges to a nice smooth curve. Stain and finish, at the same time staining and finishing two ½″-

For the miniaturist contemplating the execution of a drugstore, this soda-fountain backdrop by Mary Kopriva presents a world of ideas. Barbara Molteni of Allenwood, New Jersey, made all the luscious dainties. All are available at Jean Johnson Miniatures. (*Photograph by Muller Studio*)

Mary Kopriva made this display case, and Barbara Molteni prepared the cakes for
Jean Johnson Miniatures. (*Photograph by Muller Studio*)

Another soda-fountain backdrop shows the infinite varieties possible.

wide pieces of ⅛″ wood to form the end pieces of the counter. These will be the end supports, same height as the height of the counter.

We will use ⅟₃₆″ molding to finish the counter where the plexiglass meets the top and bottom. Soak the molding for five minutes in warm water; then shape around the outside of a saucepan and fasten with a rubber band. Let stand until dry, about an hour. Plexiglass (or SIG heat-forming plastic) is cut to fit bottom and top curves and anchored at each end with two pieces of ¼″ wood glued against each other, at the edge of both bottom and top, and against the end supports. Then glue ³⁄₁₆″ molding at two places on the plastic. Bend the plastic and insert between the top and bottom. Force the edge between the two pieces of ¼″-wide wood that were glued together. When the curved pieces of molding are completely dry, remove from the saucepan mold, cut to fit, and glue one inside the plexiglass and one outside. Attach wooden beads to form feet for the showcase.

The little shelf to the left of the cashier was made of gold plastic toothpicks, or toothpicks painted gold, with two pieces of wood, also painted gold, glued between the picks as shelves.

Coming into the kitchen, notice that the floor is covered with a paper resembling old oilcloth (a coat of varnish over this gives it a fine antiqued look), and it is darkened a bit by rubbing with a rag that has been soiled. The darkened areas indicate traffic patterns. The table is actually made from a slice of an old chopping block. (Patterns for butcher-block tables are provided in *Make Your Own Dollhouses and Dollhouse Miniatures*.) The metal sink is very crude and could be made without a pattern. It is lined with aluminum foil that has been darkened with a stain. Notice the dirty mop sitting atop a large tin can, the shelves with bakery supplies, and the towels on an undershelf rod.

Ms. Kopriva cast the stove in ceramic from an original iron piece, although this is hardly practical for most miniaturists. But the Victorian stove shown in *Make Your Own Dollhouses and Dollhouse Miniatures* would make a nice substitute. The hood is easily fashioned from copper foil; the bricks were handmade from clay. The overhead fan and lamps were made by Dot Rafferty of Manasquan, New Jersey. Notice that there is even a spiral of old-time flypaper hanging from the ceiling!

Bags and Boxes

In the course of making your miniature rooms, you will no doubt be attempting such subjects as bakeries, sweet shops, country stores, and our own corner drugstore. In all of these, bags will serve as an integral

Figure 34
Boxes and Bags
for Drugstore or Bakery

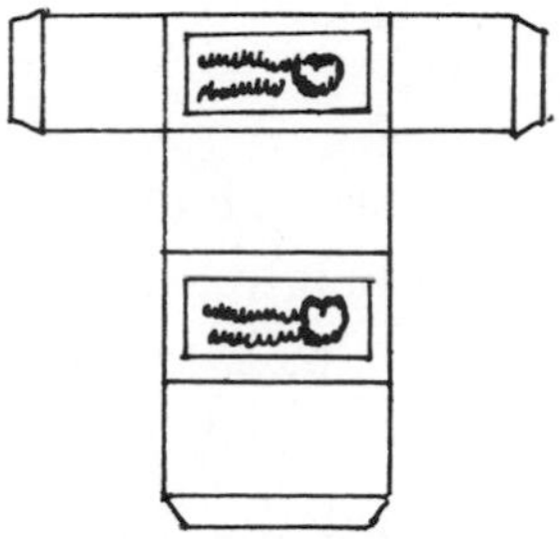

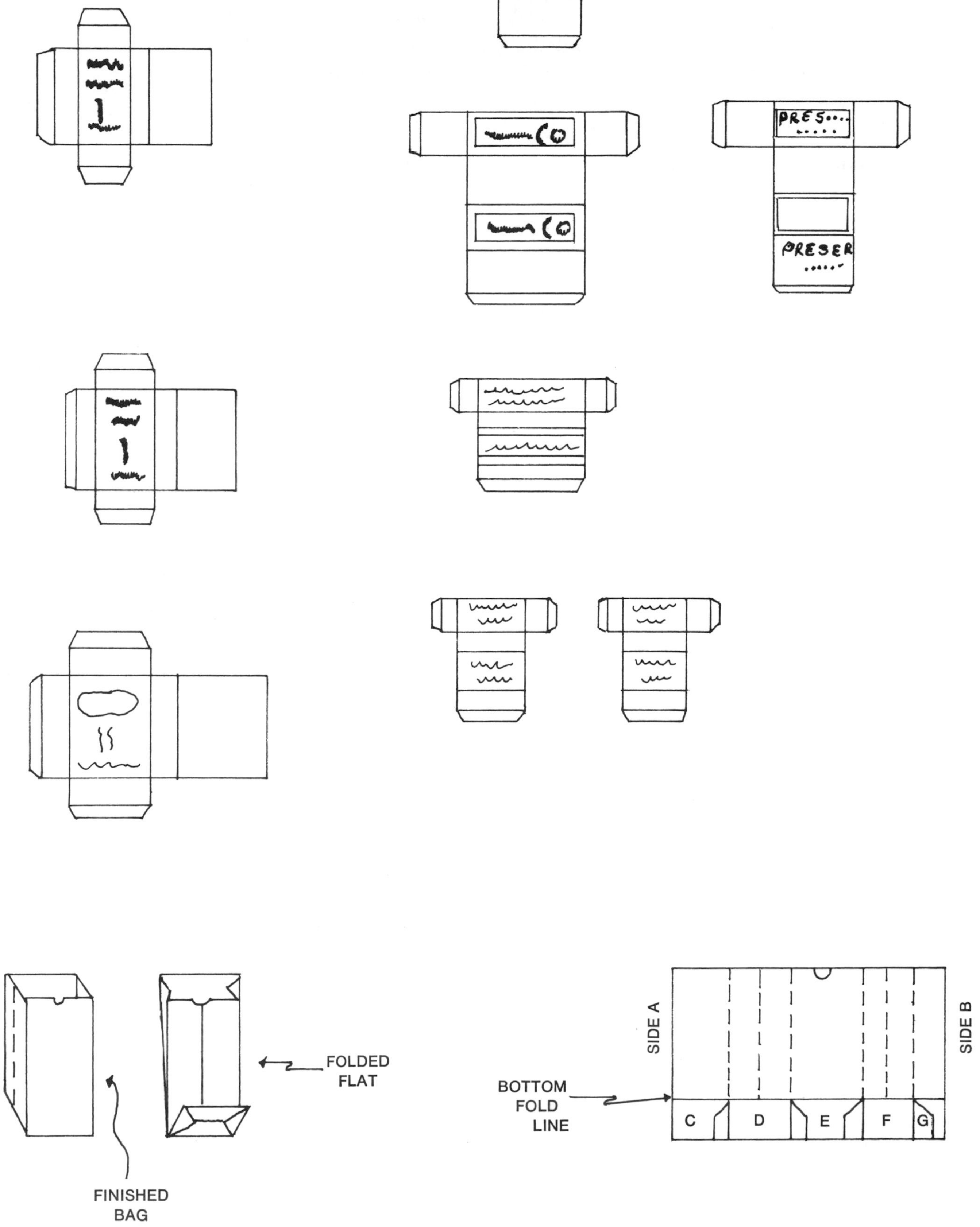

PRES····

PRESER

····

SIDE A

BOTTOM FOLD LINE

C D E F G

SIDE B

FOLDED FLAT

FINISHED BAG

part of the furnishings. Some may be bought from dealers in miniatures, but they're so simple and interesting to make that you'll want to see what you can do.

For the boxes shown at the top of figure 34, use varied colors of a medium-weight construction paper. You will want it heavy enough to make a box of some substance, but not so heavy that it can't be easily creased and folded. Trace the patterns onto your paper, then begin to letter the labels according to samples you may find in old magazines, catalogues, or books. A black felt-tip pen will give you a sharp and satisfactory black, and a set of the Mongol colored pencils made by Eberhard Faber will give you an assortment of colors. These are used first as pencils and then the design is gone over with water, giving a very fine "painted" look. Or, of course, if you are handy with a brush and have very fine-bristled examples, you could perhaps paint your own. Another possibility is to watch magazines and advertisements for colored reproductions of small packages. Cut and glue these to the boxes after they are pasted together.

To make the boxes after the labels have been drawn or glued on, cut out and score along the fold lines indicated by small arrows. Use your awl. Don't press so hard that you cut through the paper. Then simply fold in, strip a bit of glue along the end folds, fold the bottom under, and gently press together. If you are using a white-drying glue such as Crafty, I have found that it works best to make about three boxes at a time. Fold one and apply glue, then proceed to the next, and then the next. Then go back and press the bottoms against the partially dried glue, and they will stick immediately.

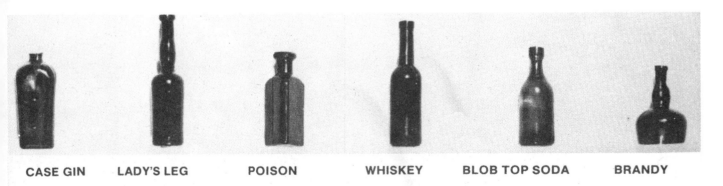

CASE GIN   **LADY'S LEG**   **POISON**   **WHISKEY**   **BLOB TOP SODA**   **BRANDY**

Tiny bottles, shown here full size, are of plastic in beautiful clear colors that look great on your drugstore shelves. They are marketed by both Miniature Mart and Molly Brody of The Golden Bough. Ms. Brody also offers a sheet of labels printed in black and white to fit the bottles, which you can color.

The smallest boxes, at extreme right, are pillboxes from the pre-scription department of a drugstore.

The bags are even simpler since they are made of paper and are easier to fold. Use brown bagging paper or whatever color letter paper you prefer. Trace and cut from the pattern given. Cut on the solid lines at *C, D, E, F,* and *G.* Fold on the dotted lines, then fold side *A* over and glue to side *B.* For the bottom, fold *D* over *F,* then *C* and *E* over these, When dry, the sides may be creased and the bottom turned up so the bags will lie flat.

13 Turn-of-the-Century Garden Party

I feel that every miniaturist who enjoys building should construct at least one diorama of an outside scene. Unlike the rather cramped plans for a dollhouse or miniature room, the setting for an outside scene must be opened up—freed of the limitations of four walls and a ceiling. It is a most refreshing exercise.

In my Victorian garden party shown here I was confined to the $\frac{1}{12}$ scale but wanted to suggest a house. Hence, I simply used a corner of the house, which, since it projects into the box, commands great interest.

One must start collecting for this project long before it actually takes shape, for some of the necessary materials are hard to come by. For my scene, for example, the background was all-important. It may be difficult to believe, but a piece of silk knit material surfaced as the background for the garden party. Notice that this is a print of Monet's painting, *Girl by a Lake*. Figures are dressed in the costumes of the period and are in perfect scale. Trees and grass work in beautifully. This, to me, was the find of the year. You might make just such a find in the wallpaper store or with a poster, but you must be looking for it.

Since as one looks toward the horizon, one sees no angles as boundaries, I did not want angles in our background. Hence, I used a medium-weight poster board—one that would curve—inside the box itself. This was cut the height of the box and long enough to fit in between the right rear corner and the front of the box, making a nice easy curve. A piece of the same material was then cut to fit the right wall of the box.

For the house, which projects into the scene, use a heavy poster board (which is the easiest to cut) or balsa or basswood sheets, which are wide enough to fit the height of the box. Cut one piece 13″ long and the height of the box and another piece 5½″ long and the height of the box.

Turn-of-the-century garden party is shown here without the box ceiling. In addition to the maid, a little bouquet of flowers was left on the chair (at left), and a hat remains on the settee (at right) to show that people were here.

All of the finishing must be done before the walls are inserted. Cut the door the size you prefer, raising it from the bottom of the wall enough to make two steps, about 1″ each, which also add to the illusion. Cut space for the window, which might be a bay such as is shown or a handsome single window. Paint the inside of the walls. I used a soft Mount Vernon green.

Now, let us go back to the inside walls. On the poster board that will be the back wall, mark off 12¼″. This will be the space to be enclosed. Cut the background material (wallpaper, material, or whatever) to fit the remainder of this wall, allowing 1″ of lap at top, sides, and bottom. Stretch over the board and staple. Paint the balance of the board (this will be inside the house) the same color you painted the inside of the walls.

Now you must find a color print that will give the illusion of looking into a house. Many of these can be found in Richard Pratt's *Golden Treasury of Early American Houses*. Mine, unbelievably, came from

Institutions Magazine, a monthly dedicated to the food trade! You must have something in striking color that carries the eye back as did my backdrops in Chapter 9 (page 113). Apply this to the board just as you would wallpaper. Notice that I have added sconces because this part of the wall is visible from the outside.

Cover the piece of poster board or basswood cut to fit the right wall with the background material. Staple if there is any doubt in your mind that material might be stained by paste. Glue this onto the right wall against the corner. I had a snippet of an old paisley shawl that I used for a carpet. Cut this to fit inside the two walls and glue.

I liked the idea of clapboard on the outside walls of the house (you could also use siding, shingles, brick, or brick-printed paper). Clapboard already milled comes in sheets about 9″ wide and 22″ long and is very inexpensive. Glue this onto the two walls and around the openings; then paint with white enamel (or some other finish consistent with the way you finished the walls). Add a frame around the door. Fit the bay window (or whatever window you are using) into the side wall. The two columns (½″ dowels) that I used to make a porch are a nice finish, especially when topped with a roof and metal railing that encloses some ferns.

When both walls are completely finished, they must be attached at the forward corner. This is easily done with the use of a milled piece called corner trim. Glue the two walls into the angle of the trim. Measure with your square to be sure that the angle is right. You may use a quick-drying glue for this, but it's difficult since you must hold the two walls into the angle. The easiest way, I found, was to use decorator's adhesive (Vogue "Stickum"), which holds immediately. Then paint the corner.

Now you must have grass. By far the easiest, but not the most effective, is the artificial grass offered in hobby shops for HO enthusiasts. The most effective, which comes in a dozen different shades, is a

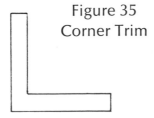

Figure 35
Corner Trim

AVAILABLE FROM "CHUCK" NEWLAND
IN ANY SIZE

Two projecting walls to suggest a house are then slipped in over the background. The walls have been entirely finished.

fine-grade foam offered by Architectural Model Supplies (see Appendix). Simply spread the bottom of the box with a thin glue (Yes, glue seems to be the best for this.) and sprinkle the foam over to cover. Press down with your hands, allow to dry, and then gently brush off the excess. For more varied ground cover, use medium- and coarse-grade ground foam.

The two house walls are slipped into the box corner as shown in the photo, fitting exactly over the rug. In my box, I even placed a Queen Anne chair just inside the door, with two steps inside to help a visitor step down. These were stained mahogany, whereas the outside steps are cut from ½″ balsa wood and painted white. Be sure they lap over the sides of the door at least ½″.

If you are not a real expert, I believe that you would be wise to order the bay window from Howard Pierce at The Workshop (see Appendix); it is a work of art. You have a choice of trims. It comes with a window seat, and it measures 5⅞″ in height by 7⅝″ in width. The window seat is 1½″ deep. I hung a little Japanese wicker birdcage in the window and made a paisley cushion for the window seat. If you

The walls, which are now in place, present a glimpse of the room inside. If you wish to add a porch, this would be done before the walls are set.

have selected a really good photo in perspective for the back wall, you'll find the glimpse through the window and the door is enchanting.

For the outside, I have used Victorian pewter furniture made by Ken Ewer of Colonial Craftsmen of which there is no finer. Paint it white. Some tin-can furniture may be used here, as witness my little table at right. This was made from a tomato-paste can, because the diameter of the can seemed to best fit the daintiness of the party. If this seems too small (it is too small to hold the cakes, cups, and tea set that are in our photo), a soup can is the next best size. Tin-can furniture is an absorbing hobby, and once you try your hand with this simple little table, you'll want to make many other pieces. The basic work is the same.

You'll need a few tools:

Straight-cut shears with spring return, or small tin snips
Awl or an ice pick
Long needle-nosed pliers for curling, or use special curling tools
   that are available

Gloves to prevent cuts when cutting and curling the tin
Grease pencil for marking the cuts
Hammer to flatten the cuts over the edge
Good can opener

For a coffee table, I wanted a height of about 1½″ more or less. Thus, with your can opener, cut the clean can around about 1¾″ from the bottom, which has not had the end cut out. With your shears or tin snips, cut out the seam. Mark ⅛″ strips all around the can as shown on our template in figure 36; then cut on these marks to the top of the can. The strips must be as straight as you can make them, and cut all in one direction—to the right if you are right handed, left if you are left handed.

You may have a lip, or edge, at the top of the can. This is particularly nice in making a table. If you don't want it, however, just use your needle-nosed pliers and bend each strip down over the lip so that the top is flat. (Be sure to wear your gloves!) You'll find that the strips are sharp while cutting, but after painting the edges are dulled.

With your grease pencil, mark off each group of strips. We are going to use eleven strips for each leg. Curling tools from Maid of Scandinavia (see Appendix) come in three sizes—⅛″, ³⁄₁₆″, and ¼″—with handles similar to screwdrivers, but your needle-nosed pliers will do as well. We are using ⅛″ curls on this table. The center strip of each group is the center of the leg. Curl up the bottom about three curls. Using the pliers, pull two strips on each side of this center one to meet the center. Tie tightly with wire, baggie ties, or tin strips. Bend first the one closest to the center, then the next one out slightly as shown in the drawing, and then fasten again with wire or other material. Curl up the four ends.

You now have three strips on each side of the leg. With the pliers, slightly turn each strip at the edge of the table toward the leg; then curl up the end. Repeat on the other side. Repeat along the edge of the can until all strips are used. If you measured correctly, on a soup can you should have about sixty-six strips, which would make six legs and produce a very elaborate table. Or, you could cut the strips a bit wider (or use a smaller can) and come up with forty-four strips, which would make four legs. Or, use more curls on each side of each leg. Or, use a smaller can.

The garden is the finishing touch for this box. I wanted to see a walk lead from the door to the side of the house so that the house would not seem constructed without plans for entering and exiting.

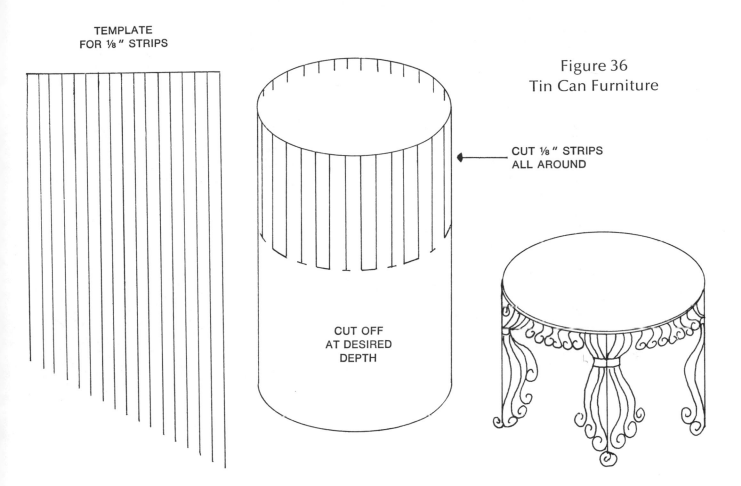

TEMPLATE FOR ⅛″ STRIPS

CUT ⅛″ STRIPS ALL AROUND

CUT OFF AT DESIRED DEPTH

Figure 36
Tin Can Furniture

You might try a variety of paths—brick, sandpaper (which looks like gravel), or the tiny white rocks that are sold as "ballast" in model-railroad shops. Directions for others are provided in *Make Your Own Dollhouses and Dollhouse Miniatures.* I decided upon stepping stones and used ordinary modeling clay of the type that comes in ¼-pound sticks like margarine and in several colors—white, gray, terra-cotta, or red.

Cut off a good ¼″ slice from the stick. With the rolling pin or a bottle or glass, roll this out on waxed paper from the center and in all directions to an irregular shape such as a stepping stone about ¹⁄₁₆″ thick. Lay on the grass where your path should go.

Trees

Trees are our next concern. The trees offered in miniature-railroad departments are too small for a ¹⁄₁₂-scale scene. But Architectural Model Supplies (see Appendix) make trees to be used by architects for

Tree shapes representing every conceivable variety of tree are shown in these two photographs, flat as they were shipped. They are of a pliable metal that is easy to work with. (*Photograph by Architectural Model Supplies, Inc.*)

Metal tree structures are pulled and bent into the shapes desired. Even shrubs may be made. The covering material, a sort of web, is then cut to fit and applied to the branches with glue. Then, thinned glue is dabbed on the covering material and ground foam in shades of green is sprinkled on. (*Photograph by Architectural Model Supplies, Inc.*)

The finished trees, as shown in these two photographs, have been "articulated," that is, bent and pulled into three dimensions, then covered with foam to represent foliage. Indispensable for any outdoor scene or for "planting" your dollhouse. (*Photograph by Architectural Model Supplies, Inc.*)

their models, and these are perfect. These are metal structures packaged flat, ready to articulate (bend) into three dimensions to make finished trees.

Materials Needed for This Project

Appropriate size and quantity tree structures

Covering material and ground foam

Glue (either contact cement or rubber cement)

Piece of foam or corrugated board with holes in which to stand finished trees until dry

The trees are primed and painted, ready to use; large ones such as 8T 90 and 8T 92 come in three sections that must be soldered together with a soldering iron. Prime and paint after soldering. Bend the branches to the desired shape; then spread out the covering material thinly and cut with scissors to approximate the amount needed to cover the branches. Tip the branches with a bit of glue; then apply the covering material. Trim off the excess covering material; then apply thin glue and sprinkle on the foliage. The glue doesn't have to be evenly spread; just dab it on.

The garden and trellis at top would make a most interesting miniature room and provide fine opportunity to exercise one's own imagination. (*Photograph by Architectural Model Supplies, Inc.*)

Detail at bottom shows a standard rose with a shrub in the back and ground cover. (*Photograph by Architectural Model Supplies, Inc.*)

My little pruned boxwood tree at the corner of the house is much simpler. Purchase a 1½″ and a 1″ styrofoam ball. Thread onto a ⅛″ dowel, the small one at the top and the larger one about 1½″ down. Tamp modeling clay into a jar. The one shown was imported by Pamela Schoenborn from Tokyo (see Appendix). Paint balls and dowel dark green. When dry, coat with thinned glue and roll in a mixture of three different shades of ground foam from Architectural Model Supplies. Rethread the balls on the dowel, and then stand in the jar.

There are many ramifications to this idea. Instead of projecting into the scene at an angle, for example, the house might stand squarely against the back wall—although you'll find this is not as interesting.

Instead of carrying the eye through the window and to the scene beyond in perspective, you might cut a window in the back wall also and mount an outdoors scene against that. This gives you a chance to build the inside window trim on the back wall, making another point of interest. Try several ideas!

14 Kakuma–
Japanese Sitting Room

This will be one of the most fascinating rooms you undertake, for there is a simplicity about it that makes for perfection. First of all, the exteriors of Japanese homes are never painted, the weathered boards being left dull and somber. Thus, the outside of your box may be finished in simple stain, applied and then after fifteen minutes or so wiped off, or antiqued according to the directions on the antiquing-fluid cans.

Interiors are distinguished mostly by stained wood, simplicity of style, and purity of finish.

In addition, nearly all Japanese rooms are square. But since we preach that the rules may be broken if our reasons are valid, and since I wanted to keep my boxes uniform for display purposes, I used my regular box, 21″ × 10½″, which gave me a lovely room but presented some most amusing problems.

First, you'll need a background since all Japanese rooms have sliding walls that bring the outdoors inside. The Japanese do not suffer from cold as we do. Moreover, inside the house they wear much warmer clothes than we do. At winter parties, the sliding walls may be left open to the garden, where there may be snow on the ground.

So, we must have the background to look out upon. Be searching for scenes of Japan that are large enough to cover the back and side walls. If you can't find any 20″ illustrations, it will be quite all right to piece two scenic photos together since the sliding wall will hide the seam and the fact that the photos don't exactly match. However, I found one in the Time-Life book of Japanese foods and another in a magazine that fit beautifully. You will also find some posters with lovely Japanese scenes at about a dollar. Once you begin searching in earnest, you'll find some in fine color.

Seal (or fill) the back and side walls of your box; then hang the scenes as you would wallpaper. Be sure to use your brayer here (as you

Japanese sitting room in a rather formal home. Notice the geta, or sandals, at the door for donning when the shoes are removed. The rice-paper screens slide in tracks on the floor and ceiling panels above.

should in any wallpapering job) so that the paper goes on absolutely smooth. Allow to dry.

You don't actually need to lay a floor over the bottom of the box since tatami mats can be used to cover the floor. In Japan the floors are usually made of rough boards with no finish. However, you never know when you may want to use the box for something else, so I consider laying a nice floor a bit of insurance. Adult-size tatami mats, made from finely woven grass, are uniformly 3′ × 6′; hence, miniatures will be 3″ × 6″.

We begin by measuring a space of 1″ between shoji screens (wooden frames covered on one side with white rice paper) that will be

Figure 37
Japanese Parlor-Kakuma

SCALE—¼ OF 1/12

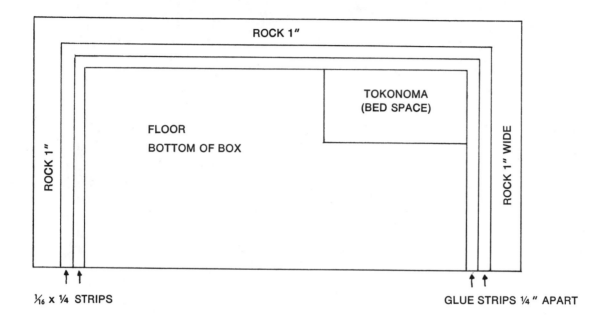

ROCK 1"

ROCK 1"

ROCK 1" WIDE

TOKONOMA
(BED SPACE)

FLOOR
BOTTOM OF BOX

¹⁄₁₆ x ¼ STRIPS

GLUE STRIPS ¼" APART

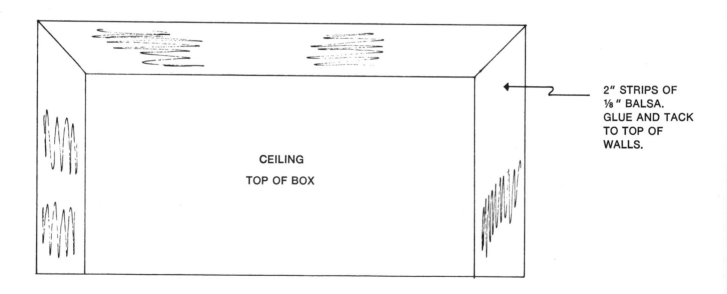

CEILING
TOP OF BOX

2" STRIPS OF
⅛" BALSA.
GLUE AND TACK
TO TOP OF
WALLS.

Japanese peasant room, constructed by Geil Butler. Crooked beams and odd-shaped timbers are used. The fence, or *sodegaki*, closest to the house is made of tree branches tied together. The one around the garden is made of rough-cut unfinished wooden boards mounted on two crosspieces, alternating one board on one side, then the next on the other side. (*Photograph by Don Barber Studio*)

placed on three sides of the room and outdoors. Almost every Japanese room is reached by way of a small walkway or veranda, and we want to create the illusion of one. Using ¼″-wide strips of ⅟₁₆″ wood, glue these on the ⅟₁₆″ side on the 1″ mark, and then glue two more of these at ¼″ intervals as shown. These are the tracks in which the shoji screens slide. When the glue is completely dry, fill the 1″ space between the tracks and the outside wall with tiny white rock chips (ballast from the mini-railroad department is exactly the right size) to the top of the outside track (¼″). This is the walkway around the outside of the room,

Japanese artifacts collected in Tokyo, shown full size. The lovely screen at the back is one of a set, hand painted. Before it is a child's toy propped upright in a box of hand-lettered books. At the other side of the screen is one of a set of rosewood tables used to display vases. At front, left to right, is a screen placed before the bed space when someone is sleeping, before it a doll 1½″ high in ceremonial dress. Next is a hibachi with teakettle carved from rosewood, a pair of geta, or sandals, a tiny doll seated at a go board, a *tobako-bon*, or smoking set, a tea set carved from wood, and books 1″ high, hand painted and hand lettered.

a sort of passageway called the *iri-kawa*, which comes between the room and the veranda.

To secure the top of the screens, the Japanese sometimes hang a heavy beam (in the 1/12 scale it would be about ½″ square) from the ceiling after cutting grooves in it in which the screens fit. In a box this size, however, this seems over large; so to secure the top of the screens, I cut pieces of 1/8″ balsa 2″ wide the length of the two sides and the back of the box, allowing for mitered corners. Miter the corners; then glue the strips to the top edge of the box, fastening first with glue and then with ½″ brass tacks. Secure the mitered corners with strips of masking tape as shown. Stain these strips, as well as the tracks and the floor, with a natural or fruitwood stain. One shouldn't use a high gloss in Japanese rooms. If you prefer a bit of a gloss, try a coat of Mona Lisa decoupage satin finish over the stain.

After you make one of the shoji screens, the remainder will be easy. First, measure your rooms carefully, making allowances for the screens to overlap on all three walls about 1″. One screen will go in the outside track and one on the inside so they can slip past one another. The height must be a snug fit from the floor to the 2″ pieces at the top of the box. Notice that at the top a ⅜″ strip of ¹⁄₁₆″ balsa is called for, but you would be wise to make this strip about ⅝″ wide and the side supports about ¼″ longer at the top so that you can then trim these off for an exact fit. The natural "give" of the balsa wood seems to provide just what's necessary for holding the screens at the top; another set of tracks at the top doesn't work well. Secured in this way, all one has to do to remove a screen is to bend it a little and out it comes.

Rice paper can be found at the local art stores. It comes plain and sometimes, as you may notice in the photos, with a sort of design imbedded in the paper. Mine seemed to be a sort of maple leaf in soft brown and green. I paid three dollars for a sheet about a yard square, which would be enough to divide among three or four friends. Pamela Schoenborn, who shops for me in Tokyo, was shocked at the price I paid, saying that it is much cheaper there—but it is often hard to find.

Stain the strips and the panel at bottom, sand, then stain again. You don't want gloss, but you *do* want a very fine finish. Glue the side strips to the base panel, leaving ¼″ space at the bottom to permit the screen to drop into the track. Glue in the strip at the top (figure 38, *A*) and the *B* strip about 3″ below, using butt joints, they're stronger than mitered joints for the top. Note that the side strips go *over* the base panel, but the *A* and *B* strips go between the strips at top. It is well to fasten these with a tiny bit of masking tape until the glue dries; there is no other way to hold them together.

While they are drying, cut a piece of rice paper to fit from the top of the screen to just over the top of the bottom panel and overlapping on the side strips enough to make it secure. Glue. Let dry under weights. When this is dry, carefully turn it over to give access to the right side of the screens. Then cut the little muntins, which have been stained, and glue in as shown. Some shoji screens use only perpendicular muntins; others use them in cross fashion as we show in our draw-

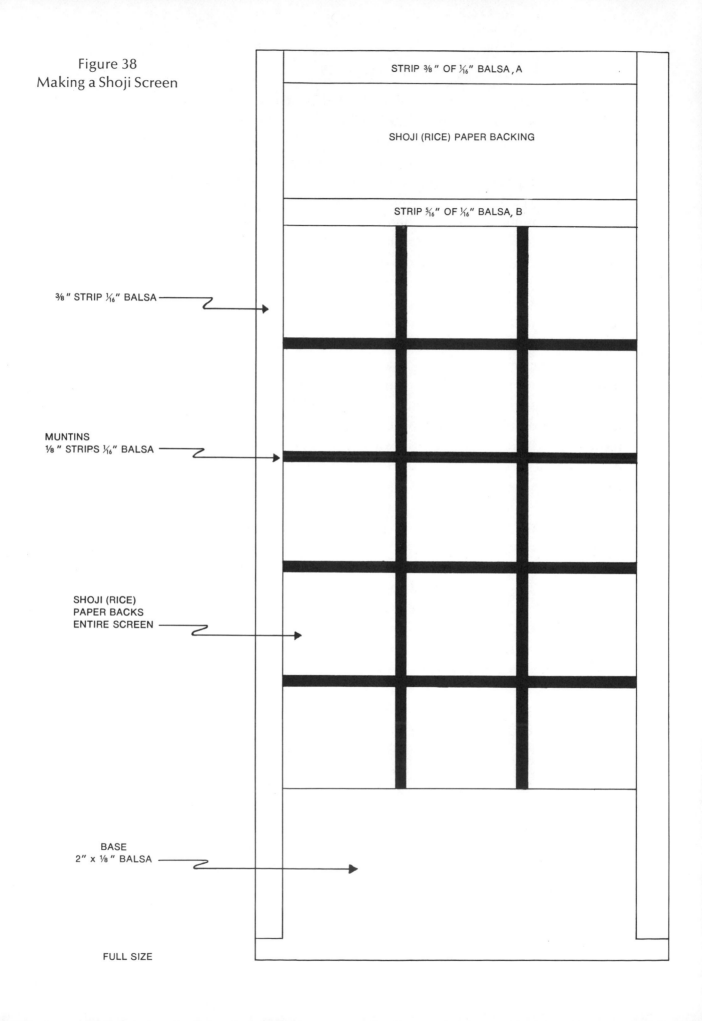

Figure 38
Making a Shoji Screen

STRIP ⅜″ OF ½₆″ BALSA, A

SHOJI (RICE) PAPER BACKING

STRIP ⅝₆″ OF ½₆″ BALSA, B

⅜″ STRIP ½₆″ BALSA

MUNTINS
⅛″ STRIPS ½₆″ BALSA

SHOJI (RICE)
PAPER BACKS
ENTIRE SCREEN

BASE
2″ x ⅛″ BALSA

FULL SIZE

ing. Some use only horizontal. I used both in this room so that you might judge the effect. In an adult-size room, of course, the screens would be finished on both sides; but since we are to see only the one side in our room, it is not necessary to finish the outside.

I wanted one permanent corner (nonsliding) to sort of anchor the walls, and since most Japanese rooms of the upper classes include a wall with a scene painted on it, I used one of the little screens published by the Charles E. Tuttle Company—out of print now but frequently found in bookstores with old books or in antique shops.

These measure 6″ by almost 13″. If you utilize the center bend on which they fold, the screen will fit into the outer track on two sides, rounding a corner. It is not, however, high enough. So using the shoji-screen technique (illustrated) I built mine up about 2¼″, or enough to meet the roof overhang. This was just a personal quirk, not at all necessary if you don't have the screens since the regulation shoji screen may well be used. However even though you don't have the screens, you may find an illustration that seems appropriate, and this may be mounted on mat board to make a permanent corner of any size you desire. Build up at the top with the shoji-screen technique to meet the ceiling.

The scroll is often hung in this permanent corner. Tiny shelves are often affixed to the screen to hold prized pieces of pottery. In the 3″ (3′ in adult size) space between the top of the screen and the muntins, prized things are often hung, such as my collection of tiny ivory hand-carved combs, which may be seen on the left wall. The characters on the right wall are from an old poem and mean "Welcome."

The rectangular space at the rear right corner of the room is the *tokonoma*, or bed space. In adult size, this is a hollow box about 6″ in depth from the floor, so we will simply build a box of ⅛″ balsa wood, the size of a tatami mat with butted corners, stained and rubbed to a soft glow. A tatami mat is placed atop this dais, then a tufted sort of comforter. This, together with a flat pillow, make up the bed. The comforter may be picked up, rolled, and stored in a cabinet by the day, or it may be left as is.

Tatami mats, the floor coverings upon which the Japanese eat, live, and sleep, are very carefully made of straw. In adult-size Japanese houses, these mats are bound together in thicknesses of about 2″. Such material is almost impossible to find here, although one occasionally comes across table place mats of straw or grass that might be used. Coarse burlap will give a similar effect. Since the cost of shipping a real tatami mat (3′ × 6′) was prohibitive, this idea was discarded until that lovely

Figure 39
Tatami Mat Arrangements

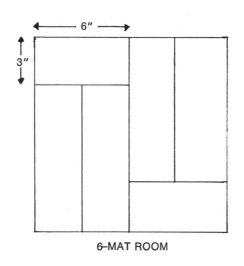

6–MAT ROOM

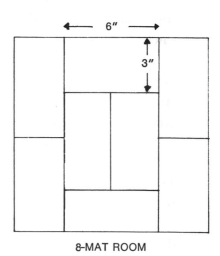

8–MAT ROOM

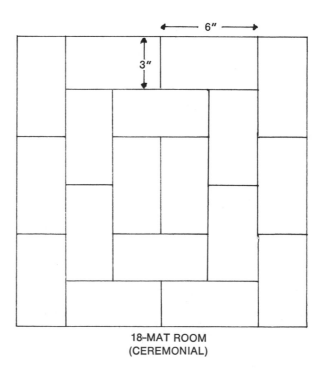

18–MAT ROOM
(CEREMONIAL)

lady who shops for me in Tokyo came up one day with a small beach mat of exactly the right scale in woven grass! Any coarse material used for the mats (including the authentic grass) ravels excessively when cut. If you will mark off the dimensions of the mat and then run a double line of any clear glue along your mark, when dry it can be cut without raveling. The mats are then bound with a narrow strip of black or other dark color; double-fold bias tape is exactly right. I stitched mine with the sewing machine; it could be done by hand or even glued down just as well.

Rooms are invariably sized to accommodate mats in even numbers —two, four, four and one half (the half mat is apparently used to make things fit), six, eight, ten, twelve, and so on. A room is referred to as a two-mat room, a six-mat room, and so on.

Notice that in the room in the photograph, because it is oblong rather than square, I was unable to use mats in the way the Japanese use them. After much experimentation, I simply made three mats to exactly fit our floor and let it go at that.

In the square Japanese room, the corners of the mats are never allowed to come together; mats are arranged so that the corners of two mats abut against the side of the third (see figure 39). The mats should fit tightly so that, as we mentioned before, a finished floor is not needed.

Cut paper patterns until you have the size mat you wish to use; then cut from your material and bind with bias tape.

Glossary of Japanese House Terms

Futam   The sleeping mat that, laid down anywhere with a quilt, constitutes a bed

Geta   Small black-lacquered sandals for a geisha

Go   The popular game in Japan, played with stones.

Hibachi   The pot that holds the fire—always hot in the corner of a Japanese room to heat water for tea

Hina dolls   Lovely figures prized by collectors, which represent court figures of the emperor and empress

Ikebana   The Japanese art of flower arranging

Irassharmash'ta!   Welcome!

Iri-kawa   Space between the wall and the veranda or between walls and walk

Kakuma   The Japanese parlor

Koto   Japanese harp, an instrument of thirteen strings

Shoji screens   Screens that form the outside walls of rooms

The chest and mirror shown at center rear are beautiful lacquerwork in black decorated in red and gold, judged to have been made around 1900. Other pieces are modern. The bed screen at left is coromandel work by Charlene Larsen, and the tall instrument is a Japanese harp. At front, left to right, is a hibachi of soft green metal and a lamp similar to those shown at the rear. The little doll is seated at a 3"-long black-lacquer table decorated in gold, and the container at right is another hibachi, carved from wood and containing ashes.

Shoji-no-kami   Rice paper
Soroban   Abacus
Tatami   Grass mats, 3′ × 6′, that cover the floor
Tobako-bon   Smoking set with holder and ash container
Tokonoma   Bed space; the area where the scroll is hung
Zabuton   Cushions around the table, in summer made of straw, in winter of silk

It is interesting to study the photographs since our shopper in Tokyo reports that the old folks who make these lovely miniatures are rapidly disappearing from the scene and the younger generation does not seem to be interested in carrying on the tradition.

Holiday miniatures executed by Japanese artists are shown full size. The two pieces at left resembling candlesticks are actually hung on each side of the door-way to ward off evil spirits. The birdcage contains a miniature swallow, thought to bring good luck to the home.

If you have access to a shopper in this lovely country, however, another possibility suggests itself. The pottery stall shown on page 182 is only one of some twenty-four or thirty that are made, consisting of every sort of stall known in Japan and reminding us of the shallow shops that were made in England, although these are much more minute. The pottery stall, for example, is only 5″ high at the back—obviously less than the $\frac{1}{12}$″ scale, and the tiny plates are in this proportion—but imagine how lovely a street scene showing the stalls would be!

The accessories, because they are so small and so simple, will contribute a great deal to your enjoyment of the building of the Japanese room. The all-purpose table that occupies the center of the room and is used for playing games, entertaining, reading, and eating, is shown full size in figure 40. The top is cut 3″ square from a piece of $\frac{1}{2}$″ pine or basswood, and for decoration a ridge is routed out about $\frac{1}{8}$″ from the top. If you don't have a router such as the Dremel instrument, a bit of $\frac{1}{8}$″ molding glued on here will serve the same purpose: to break up the stark look of the wood.

Close-up of a pottery stall shows everyday and ceremonial plates. The tiny case at front center is just 1″ high, the stall about 5″.

The four legs are then cut from ½″ wood, ¾″ square, and glued onto the top at the corners. Finish with several coats of black lacquer, sanding lightly between coats. About four coats will give you a nice finish.

Go is the most popular game in Japan; it is played by young and old, at all levels of society, and newspapers even carry go columns, as our papers carry bridge columns. The little go table imported from Japan is cut from ½″ pine or basswood, and the corners and other edges are sanded off just a bit so there are no sharp edges. The top is then marked in ⅛″ squares as shown, and ¼″ beads are attached as legs. I used a half bead above the ¼″ bead so as to give it some sort of setting and raise the table for ease in sitting.

The piece received from Japan was left in natural wood, the squares marked at ⅛″ intervals in India ink. In actual play, small stones were used, but in my set the men were tiny slices from a ⅛″ dowel, half of them painted black. The boxes in which the stones are shaken are ⅝″ beads, hollowed out with a drill or a knife. Tiny flat pieces of wood are then cut to make lids for the boxes, and the entire thing is stained a rich, dark brown.

The *tobako-bon,* as might be guessed from the sound of the words, is a Japanese smoking set. Shown in the photograph in actual size, it is

Figure 40

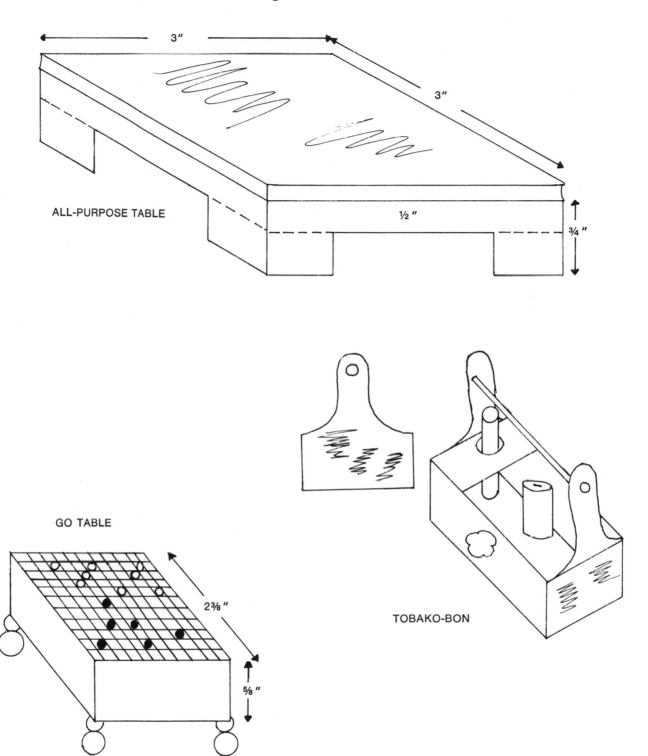

ALL-PURPOSE TABLE

3"

3"

½"

¾"

GO TABLE

2⅜"

⅝"

TOBAKO-BON

cut from $\frac{1}{16}''$ wood and has glued in at one end a tiny $\frac{3}{8}''$ shelf with a hole in the center. In this hole, in the set that came from Japan, a $1''$ piece of bamboo was inserted; this is the holder for whatever one is smoking. The larger receptacle in the center of the set is an ash container, which is cut from a $\frac{1}{2}''$ dowel. In my set, which was lacquered a rich, deep umber and sprinkled with flakes of gold, the ash container was painted a turquoise blue, the black then painted gray to simulate ashes. A delightful piece! A $\frac{1}{16}''$ dowel is inserted in holes in each handle to provide a handhold.

One last accessory for your Japanese room will be the *zabuton,* or cushions on which the family sit around the table as they eat, visit, or play games. These are made of straw in the summer and silk in the winter, but after my troubles with raveling in making the tatami mats, I wanted nothing to do with making small straw cushions. Mine are made of soft green silk on one side and velvet on the other in a bright blue— two colors that tie in with the screen used as a wall in the right rear corner. Cut the material in $3''$ squares, the size of the table; sew two pieces together leaving a $\frac{1}{8}''$ margin and you will have exactly the right size—just a bit smaller than the table. Stitch on three sides; then stuff with hair combings, $\frac{1}{8}''$ polyurethane cut to fit, or any other material you have on hand. The cushions are stitched with the right sides of the material together, of course, and then turned before stuffing. Also, they should be pressed before stuffing.

Stitch up the fourth side with tiny stitches; then secure the stuffing in the center with either a cluster of French knots or of beads. Place the cushions around the table.

15 Fourth-of-July Picnic, ca.1914

If you have (or lately had) a youngster in the seventh or eighth grades, you've had some experience in constructing cycloramas and dioramas. This is an old, old art that has recently been revived in order to show children how they can create a scene in a small space.

To the miniaturist, this art is timely, since it allows one to capture a memory or to record a happening that could not have taken place inside a miniature room. When we plan to create an outdoor scene, we must consider other requirements, since we try to capture an entire slice of life rather than just a scene. Our possibilities, however, are endless.

Two forms are available to us; first, the cyclorama, which might be used for the miniature theater in Chapter 9 and which represents a scene or landscape in perspective on the inner wall of a cylindrical room; and, next, the diorama, a scene in miniature that is reproduced in three dimensions by placing objects, figures, and furnishings in front of a painted background. The diorama is usually viewed through a sort of peephole, which sharpens the image, and this, basically, is the form of the "poppy show" that youngsters of another generation built in a shoe box and allowed their peers to peep at for a penny a look.

Both the cyclorama or the diorama may be built in a shadow box, and I constructed my Fourth-of-July picnic (with a doff of my hat to the Bicentennial Year) the same size as I used for all my boxes—20″ long (which actually works out to about 19½″) and 10½″ high.

Then I needed a curved background—you couldn't have an outdoors scene with corners, could you?—and for this I used a fairly heavy poster board for the ground and a lighter board (rather like shirt board) for the backdrop. You must have a piece for the ground about 19½″ long and 10″ deep so as to cut the proper curve (see figure 41). The backdrop takes a piece about 28″ long and 10½″ high to make the

The first step in making a diorama is installing the background and planning for the projections. Notice how the print used carries the eye back, as though into another room. The print is pasted onto the back wall; background material is stapled to poster board.

curve (see *A*). Cover the ground piece with artificial grass from the mini-railroad department of a toy or hobby store or with shredded-foam ground cover as offered by Architectural Model Supplies (see Appendix). Then cut fourteen 1″ pieces of ¼″ square balsa. Glue these in pairs around the curve of the grass, with ⅛″ between each of the two pieces. Allow to dry thoroughly. Notice that you have constricted your usable space a bit, but you still have two nice roomy corners in which electrical equipment may be placed.

Bear in mind that this project was to be a Fourth-of-July picnic, which was always held in a park or on the village green and which traditionally was the setting for political speeches and impassioned oration. I first bought a light blue poster board for the background and then laboriously inked in a village with rolling acres and hills in the background. (I mention all this so you'll know what to avoid.) I glued little wads of cotton, pulled into cloud shapes, on the sky. It was fair, but not good. I was not happy. Then, in a little gift shop in a nearby shopping center one day (I case these regularly so as not to miss any real

A Fourth-of-July picnic in 1914 was invariably political. This one is set in a park with a poster-board background and might be slipped into a box. Vines at the two edges increase the illusion of a park. The dolls are Renwal, ca. 1945, completely jointed. Notice the hot-air balloon!

finds), I found the large posters such as young people hang on walls, on sale. There was a beautiful one titled "Harvest," which had been $3.50 but was marked down to 97¢. Watch for bargains. A perpendicular scene often will not do the job, but this was a horizontal scene mounted verti- cally in the display stand. As I whipped out the little tape measure I am never without, I realized that it was just the size I needed—30″ long and about 21″ high! I carried it home in triumph and in a matter of minutes had it trimmed and mounted on the original poster board. I used wallpaper paste and dried under weights (books) to prevent warp- ing. It was perfect and makes the loveliest background you ever saw.

When the backdrop scene is just about dry, turn it over and glue to the wrong side two 10½″ strips of ⅛″ basswood at each end—strips about ½″ or ¾″ wide. These help to keep the ends of the background erect. Dry under weights again, and then you are ready to mount your backdrop. Gently shape it into a curve and fit the bottom edge into the little pegs that you have mounted along the edge of the grass curve. You'll love it, and so will everyone else.

Figure 41
Cyclorama

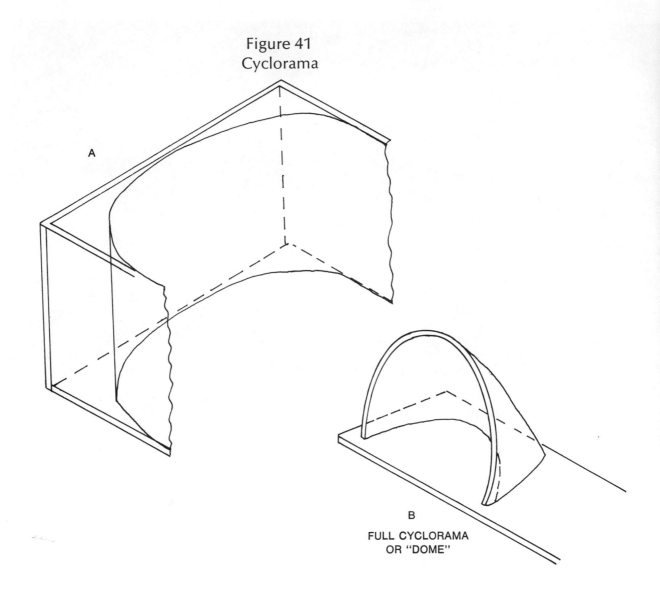

A

B

FULL CYCLORAMA
OR "DOME"

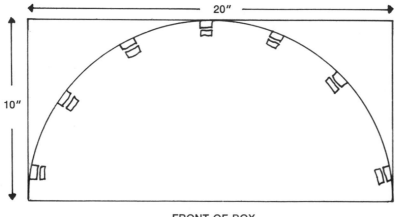

BOTTOM OF BOX
SHOWING PEGS TO HOLD BACKGROUND

20"

10"

FRONT OF BOX

C

It seems best to pass over directions for the full cyclorama or "dome" shown in figure 41, since this is much more difficult and not really practical for a shadow box such as you are making. It is usually formed from plaster and so limits your space (compare the shape to the skin of a quartered orange) that it's really hardly worth your while. Full cycloramas are rare in either mini- or full-size theaters, or in shadow boxes.

Now you are ready to plan your scene. Have the catalogue from Architectural Model Supplies at hand (see Appendix). Or, you will find many usable things in the miniature-railroad department at your hobby store, although the trees here aren't large enough for a $\frac{1}{12}$-scale scene, whereas Architectural's are. They also list streetlights, people, boats, and vehicles.

Use your imagination here. I originally worked with a plastic gazebo from the Maid of Scandinavia catalogue (see Appendix); it was the right height but not in the correct scale otherwise. Group enough trees around the back of the curve to hide the meeting of wall and grass, and be sure to make them of varying heights. For the stump, from which our candidate was to speak, I selected a nice 2″ branch and cut off a piece 2″ high—Honest John Also Ran loved getting close to the people.

His banner, which can be stretched across the scene at any angle you prefer, is a 2″ strip of sheeting with ¼″ edges pressed or stitched in. The message can be lettered on (sheeting takes marks from felt-tip pencils beautifully and a splendid assortment of colors are available), but mine was done with the little push-out letters that are bought in sheets at the stationery shop and come in a half dozen different styles.

Picnic Tables

One might use any number of designs for the picnic table, but the one shown is used in most parks and is very effective. Use ⅛″ hardwood throughout; back and seats are 1″ wide, and the legs and braces are ¼″ strips.

Materials Needed for This Project
1 length ⅛″ basswood, 1″ wide and about 3′ long
1 length ⅛″ basswood, ¼″ wide and about 2½′ long
   Wood glue
   Stain

Cut the pieces as shown in figure 42. Bevel off all edges with a bit of sandpaper; then stain and finish. Remember that this is an outdoor table; you don't want a furniture finish on it.

Figure 42
Picnic Table

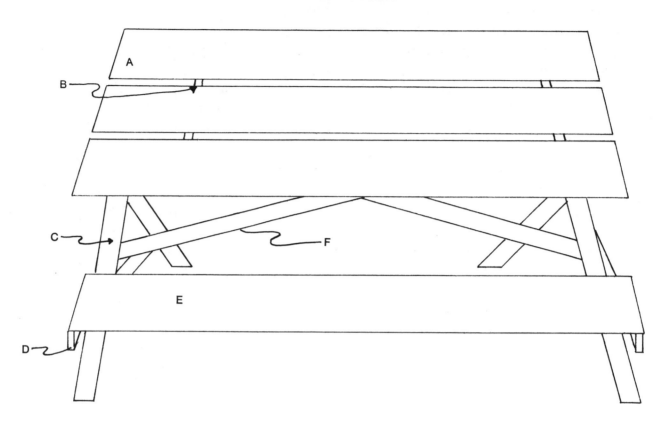

LEGS 2½" x ¼" CUT 4

TOP SUPPORTS 2¾" x ¼" CUT 2

ANGLE BRACES 2¼" x ¼" CUT 2

TOP AND SEATS 6" x 1" CUT 5

SEAT SUPPORTS
4¾" x ¼"
CUT 2

Angle off the ends of the legs and the braces; the angles I show won't be exact, but you can trim to make the table set steady after it is put together. Lay the three pieces for the top on your worktable, allowing a tiny distance between boards. Glue the top supports onto the boards with the ⅛″ edge against them; they should be about 1″ from the edges of the table top. When these are dry, check the angles on the leg ends. When these are correct, glue to the inside of the top supports. When these are dry, glue the seat supports to the outside of the legs, their tops about 1½″ up from the ends of the legs. Allow these, too, to dry; then glue the seat boards to the ends and you're finished.

Park Bench

The bench without a back becomes a very nice table to go with the other bench if the base is cut about ⅜″ taller, making the table stand about 3″ high.

Materials Needed for This Project

7 tongue depressors about 4″ long, ⅜″ wide
  Scraps of ¼″ plywood for bases
  Small tacks
  Dark green enamel

For the bench with a back, at top, cut two of *A* in figure 43. NOTE: If you look carefully at the boy seated on the bench at right in the photo, you'll notice that he leans back a bit too far. This means that the angle at the back of *A* is too great. For a straighter back, cut on the dotted line. Simply nail the tongue depressors to the bases with tiny tacks; then paint with green enamel.

The bench without a back at the bottom of the drawing is made with a base cut from *B* with three tongue depressors tacked on top. These depressors have a tendency to move on the bases as the tacks loosen up; it might be a good idea to glue a strip of wood against the top and the base on the wrong side.

Paint all with dark green enamel.

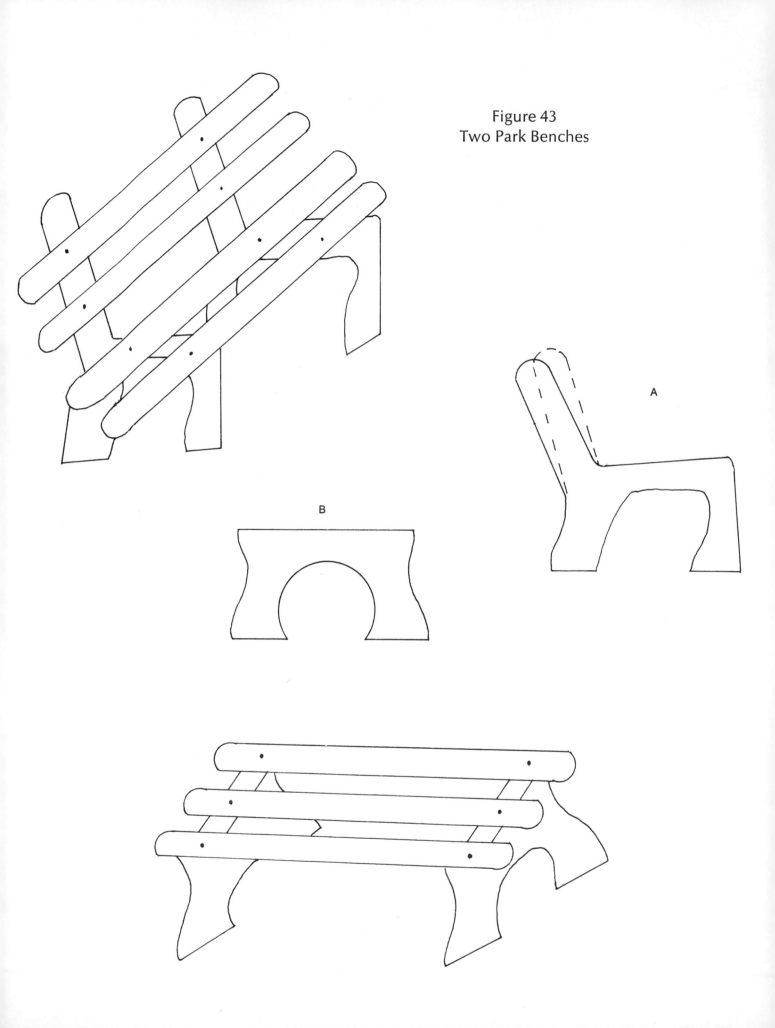

Figure 43
Two Park Benches

A

B

The placards, which were an important part of every Fourth-of-July parade, support Honest John, who is on the speaker's stump in the photo. They are made of two pieces of varied-color construction paper glued together with a swab stick or other small dowel inserted between. Letter before mounting.

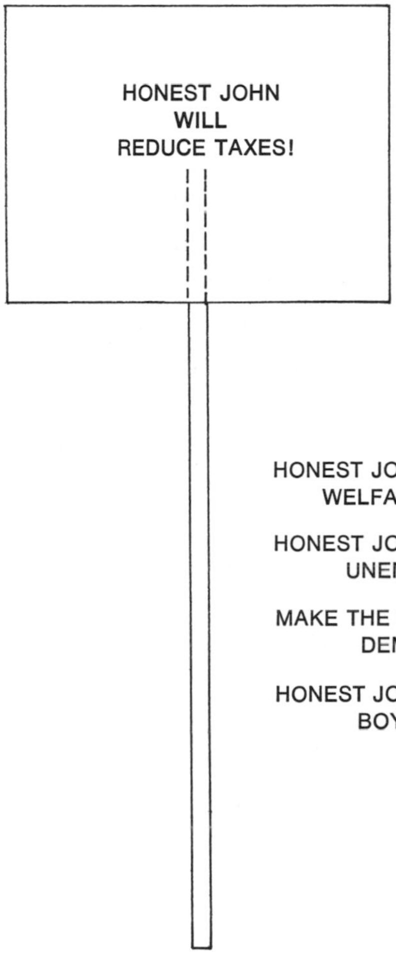

HONEST JOHN
WILL
REDUCE TAXES!

Figure 44
Placards

HONEST JOHN WILL INCREASE
WELFARE PAYMENTS!

HONEST JOHN WILL WIPE OUT
UNEMPLOYMENT!

MAKE THE WORLD SAFE FOR
DEMOCRACY!

HONEST JOHN WILL KEEP OUR
BOYS AT HOME!

16 Game Room, ca. 1950

Our game room from the opulent fifties may be the most interesting room in this collection. It is entirely original, owing none of its charm to history or period, and it relates closely to all of the things that one must have in mind when contemplating the making of a miniature room—that is, scale, decoration, appropriateness, and creativity. The accessories are fun to make, and you will learn much in the planning of this room that can be applied to rooms in your adult-size house.

I want to point out, however, how wrong one can be even when one's thinking is categorically correct. I used my regular box size—20″ × 12″ × 11″. In a room this long, one should have ample space for both a ping-pong table and a billiard table, since in adult size the first is only 5′ wide and the second less than 4′ wide. And, if you lay your room out on graph paper (something we strongly advise for every room you plan), this plan looks perfectly feasible.

But if you go ahead, you'll find yourself in trouble, for even if you reduce the size of the tables (I reduced my ping-pong table to 3″ wide and the billiard table to about the same, the length of both to about 6″, your room will accommodate nothing but the two tables and be deadly uninteresting.

First, I removed one of the tables—you might choose which you prefer to retain. This gave us space to use a little Renwal bridge set that dates from the late 1940s and is quite rare, on which I placed a backgammon board. Against the left wall, I then had room for one of Charles Graves's beautiful inlaid tables, set for a chess game, and an imposing fireplace with a chair beside it on the back wall.

Both the bridge set and the red-velvet chair are a bit under $\frac{1}{12}$ scale, but as may be seen from the photo, they fit perfectly with the other furniture and give the room a really vital, lived-in look, which is what I was trying for.

Game room, ca. 1950, shows use of full-size paper pattern as a mural. *Hina* dolls on the mantel are an import, vases are by Suzanne Ash of Mini-Things, and fireplace is by Molly Brody. The chess table and pieces are by Charles Graves, the bridge set is a Renwal collectible of about 1945. Billiard-table pattern is by Charles W. Betty. (*Photograph by Elinor Coyle*)

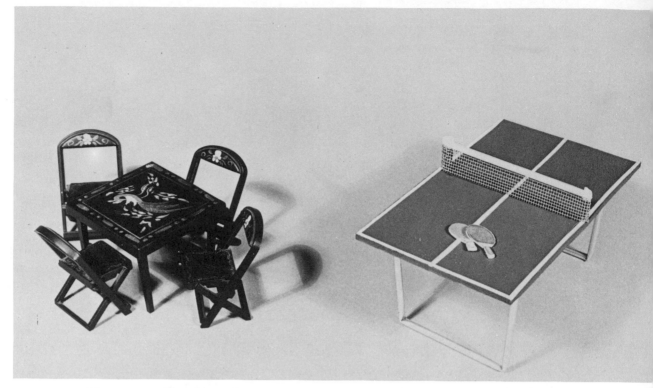

Two outstanding pieces in my game room are, at right, the ping-pong table, for which directions are given, and, at left, a Renwal plastic bridge set of the late 1940s decorated, as were many of the Renwal pieces, with colorful stenciled designs. This is actually about ¾ of the 1/12 scale but fits in nicely with the other pieces.

Even the wallpaper is a departure from the rules of scale. While dozens of patterns in the proper scale are available, this room was inspired by the find of a roll of Thibaut paper (adult-size) titled "Chinese Garden." Notice that one pattern covers the rear wall and resembles a mural. The figures are about 2½" high or less, and the pattern repeats every 15", making it possible to cut one whole scene for a 12" wall.

The companion paper, called "Bamboo," is actually a sort of cane pattern, the cane being the color of cane or bamboo, against a red background to match the garden paper. Colors throughout are beautiful—reds and golds and greens with touches of a very delicate blue here and there. The cane pattern is less than ¾" wide.

One more thing must be considered here. Unless one makes a lucky find, one must buy a whole roll of such paper and in this case it would cost $8.95. Even so, you shouldn't have any trouble parceling it out to fellow miniaturists or members of your club—I offered mine at

$1.00 per pattern in *Dollhouse and Miniature News* and disposed of two rolls within a week!

Using full-size wallpaper in a miniature room, while presenting no particular difficulties, does require a certain amount of precise measuring. First, we must make certain that the pattern is going to fit our room, so that it is, actually, presented as a mural, with a top, a bottom, and two sides. We must have no beheading of figures or top sides of buildings left hanging in the air. In this case, I fitted the side walls first because they're relatively simple, the only requirement being that both sides must meet the wall at the same point in the pattern. Cut the paper, allowing ½″ to overlap the back wall. In this instance, ordinary wallpaper paste was perfectly satisfactory. Paper each side wall, being sure to use your brayer so the paper will be smooth. You will have ½″ of paper overlap onto the back wall. Press into the corner.

Now, cut the pattern for the back wall to an exact fit. Paste and fit onto the wall. Use the brayer until any excess paste is pressed out. Be sure that the pattern is centered on the wall. Allow to dry before proceeding.

With the wallpaper on, you will want to think about the floor. Because this is a game room (I still might paint a shuffleboard court on the floor) I wanted something other than wood. The perfect answer was something I found in a hardware store called Wallcork—tiny pieces of cork pressed together in ⅛″-thick 1′ × 2′ sheets, sold four in a package. You'll only need one sheet, but you can either sell the balance to a friend or keep it for another room—it has endless possibilities. I didn't even glue mine down; I just cut it to fit and laid it against the wood floor. You can apply a coat of varnish, but I preferred mine in the natural state. Wallcork makes a fine floor for games, and a beautiful one to boot. This material would even be great for a wall cover in another room.

Shutters and Doors

Shutters and a matching louvered door make the perfect accessories for such a room, and I will give explicit directions, since you will be using these again and again both inside your miniature rooms and out.

Balsa wood is the perfect material for shutters as I make them, and it can be found in hobby shops in any thickness. You will need ¹⁄₁₆″ and ¹⁄₃₂″ for this project. Notice that I haven't given any measurements on my drawing; I have omitted these because your doors and windows will

A

E

E

B

E

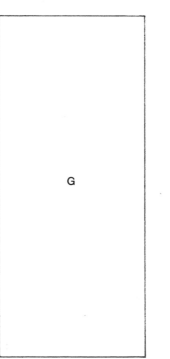

C

G

G

F

D

Figure 45
Shutters or
Louvered Doors

no doubt not conform with mine. I have used the standard 3″ width for both windows and doors and the 7″ height for the door. Adjust these measurements to fit your room; if you are making shutters or double doors, use half the width of the opening for each shutter or door. In the case illustrated, this meant 1½″ for each shutter or door 7″ in height.

Materials Needed for This Project
1 piece ¹⁄₁₆″ balsa wood, 3″ wide and 7″ long
1 piece ¹⁄₃₂″ balsa wood, 3″ wide and 7″ long
  Square of glass
  Graph paper marked in ⅛″ squares
  Doorknobs as needed
  Hinges for the shutters
  Clear-drying glue such as Tacky
  Metal-edged ruler, cork backed
  Utility knife

If you are making shutters, you will use only the top half of the door, shown in figure 45, with a ¼″ strip in the center. Cut the uprights (side pieces) ³⁄₁₆″ wide and as long as you want your shutter or door. Cut four for each door or shutter. Also from the ¹⁄₁₆″ wood, you will need a crosspiece at top to make a butt joint. Cut two for each piece. If making shutters, cut an additional two, ¼″ wide for the center piece. Cut two pieces (C) ½″ wide from ¹⁄₁₆″ wood for the center break. For a door, you will need two pieces (D) for the bottom break.

For this project, you will find that your greatest aid in keeping the slats aligned will be a square of glass fitted over a piece of graph paper marked in ⅛″ squares. In making doors and shutters, I like to use a piece of waxed paper over this; it seems to prevent the glued pieces from sticking.

Now, using the lines on the graph paper as a guide, lay out for each shutter or door two uprights. Glue in the top panel (A), the center panel (C), and the bottom panel (D). You'll find it a bit difficult to hold the joints until the glue is set; a tiny piece of masking tape across the joint will secure it. Let dry under a weight.

While this is drying, cut the louvers from ¹⁄₃₂″ wood, ¼″ wide and ⅛″ longer than the space between the two uprights (B) when glued. Cut piece G exactly as wide as the outside measurements of the two uprights and long enough to reach to the bottom of piece D and about halfway across piece C.

It is essential to remember when using balsa wood that all pieces are cut *with* the grain rather than across the grain. You will have

Figure 46
Tips on Cutting Balsa Wood

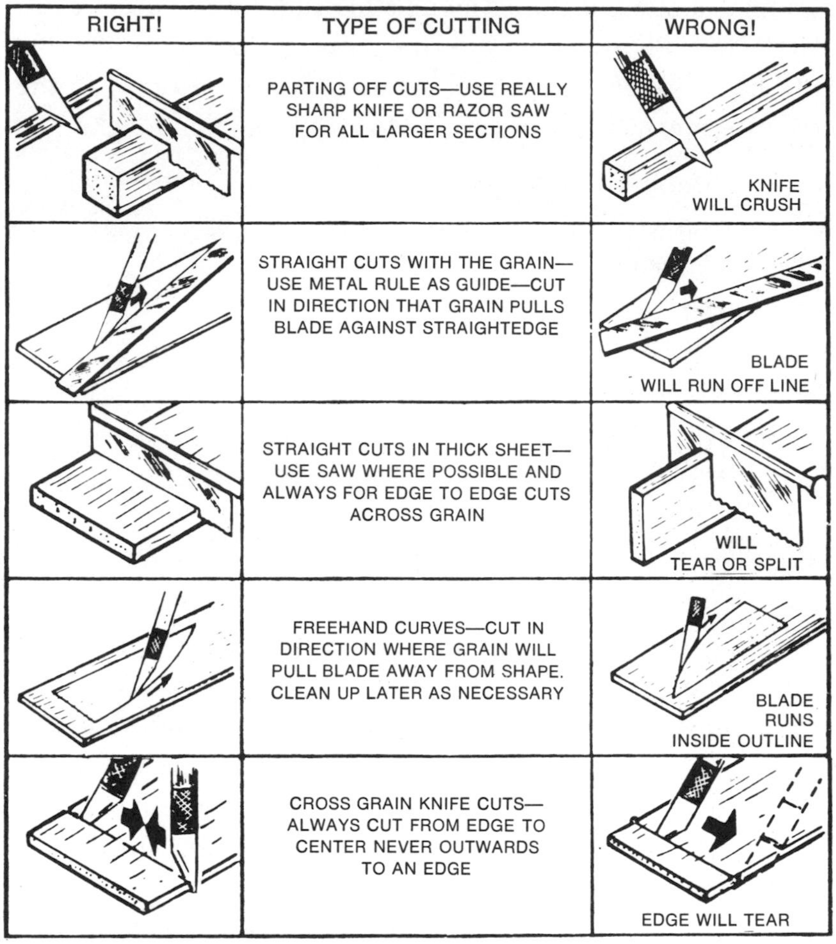

RIGHT!	TYPE OF CUTTING	WRONG!
	PARTING OFF CUTS—USE REALLY SHARP KNIFE OR RAZOR SAW FOR ALL LARGER SECTIONS	KNIFE WILL CRUSH
	STRAIGHT CUTS WITH THE GRAIN—USE METAL RULE AS GUIDE—CUT IN DIRECTION THAT GRAIN PULLS BLADE AGAINST STRAIGHTEDGE	BLADE WILL RUN OFF LINE
	STRAIGHT CUTS IN THICK SHEET—USE SAW WHERE POSSIBLE AND ALWAYS FOR EDGE TO EDGE CUTS ACROSS GRAIN	WILL TEAR OR SPLIT
	FREEHAND CURVES—CUT IN DIRECTION WHERE GRAIN WILL PULL BLADE AWAY FROM SHAPE. CLEAN UP LATER AS NECESSARY	BLADE RUNS INSIDE OUTLINE
	CROSS GRAIN KNIFE CUTS—ALWAYS CUT FROM EDGE TO CENTER NEVER OUTWARDS TO AN EDGE	EDGE WILL TEAR

much trouble if you try to cut small pieces across the grain, on almost any wood.

Now, starting at the bottom, glue piece G onto the frame. Side edges should exactly meet as should the bottom. The top should overlap piece C about ¼″. Dry under a weight. When the glue has set, start the louvers by running a very fine line of glue across the bottom of piece A. Run a very fine line of glue down the inside edges of piece B. Lay the louvers (E) against the top and press against the side uprights (B). Trace a fine line of glue along the bottom of the first louver and press the next louver in, overlapping about ¹⁄₁₆″. Continue on down to the center panel, piece C, or if you are making shutters, to the ¼″ strip in the center. Then continue on down to the bottom. A panel in the bottom half of the door doesn't seem necessary to me if you are making the half-size door pictured. If you are making a full-size (3″) door, however, the bottom panel needs some ornamentation. You have cut G from $\frac{1}{16}''$ wood. Cut the two panels (F) from $\frac{1}{16}''$ wood also, about $\frac{3}{16}''$ smaller all around. Sand the edges to a bevel. Glue in the center of panel G, making sure you glue the panel on the *outside* of the door. Lay the second frame, which by now is dry, over all this. Add another panel to G on this side of the door. Make certain that all edges are even. Dry under a weight.

F is a nice way to finish the bottom panel on a full-size door; here I used a panel to the edge in the center and a panel on each side, much as the doors in your own home are finished.

When your doors or shutters are all dry and sturdy, you will notice that on the sides and top, where the louvers are situated, the uprights don't quite meet because of the bulk made by the louvers. Cut a tiny sliver ($\frac{1}{16}''$ wide) from $\frac{1}{16}''$ wood the length needed. Drip a bit of glue into the open space with a toothpick; then force the sliver in. When this is dry, sand the edges carefully for a nice smooth finish.

You will need only hinges for the shutters. Doorknobs are nice, and there has been some use of doorknobs fastened in the center of the center panel. Search for upholstery tacks (some come with very elaborate heads) to use for the knobs, or purchase knobs from the many firms that offer them. Some are even offered with keyholes, many with elaborate escutcheons.

Ping-Pong Table

My ping-pong table is one of my dearest possessions; it comes as close to being perfect as any miniature I have ever seen. As explained before, I altered scale a bit to present a more integral room. My table is $6\frac{1}{4}''$ long $\times$ $3''$ wide, and it's perfect for this room. Use $\frac{1}{8}''$ balsa and cut to these dimensions. Sand edges carefully. Again, please note a variation from scale. Regulation-size ping-pong tables are from $\frac{1}{2}''$ to $\frac{3}{4}''$ thick. Thus, $\frac{1}{16}''$ wood would be nearer scale for the top, but this looks much too frail for the table. Again, we realize that we are artists and must adjust to rules to suit our purposes.

Materials Needed for This Project
1 length $\frac{1}{8}''$ balsa wood, $3''$ wide and about $7''$ long
1 length $\frac{3}{8}''$ balsa wood, $2''$ wide and about $2''$ long
1 length $\frac{1}{8}''$ brass or aluminum tubing, $18''$ long
1 length adhesive tape, about $7''$ long
  Small piece $\frac{1}{8}''$ mesh screen wire

2 ¾″ wire nails
Tacks or brads to fasten legs
4 ⅝″ wire nails
1 small piece ¹⁄₁₆″ wood
Utility knife
Metal-edged ruler
Dark green acrylic paint
Blue and red acrylic paint, or thin rubber

Cut the piece of ⅜″ balsa into two 1″-wide strips. Glue these to the underside of the table about ½″ from each end, centered. Dry under a weight. Paint the top and all exposed edges with dark green acrylic paint. Let dry thoroughly.

For the striping I used white adhesive tape. The center line is a bit wider on a regulation table than the border lines; I cut the tape to ⅛″ wide for the center and about ¹⁄₁₆″ wide for the borders. It's difficult to do this perfectly with a pair of scissors; it's easily done, however, if you'll cut a piece of the tape the length you need (6¼″) and press it down on your cutting board. Cut the strips of tape using a utility knife and a metal-edged ruler; then simply pull up off the board and press onto the table. Do the center strips first and then the borders. I preferred mitering the corners of the borders; since the tape is so narrow, it's no problem.

I moped around for days searching for a material for the net and wound up with—guess?—window-screen wire! The meshes are exactly the right size, and it adapts itself to our needs most satisfyingly. You may have an old window screen; if not, most hardware stores sell little packages of screen patches. Most of them aren't quite wide enough for our 4″ requirement, however. Cut the screen ⅝″ wide and 4″ long. Again, cut a strip of adhesive tape by laying it on your cutting board and cutting ¼″ wide and 4″ long. Pick up the tape and lay it across the top of the screen strip, covering the strip to half the tape width. Fold over and press hard. At the exact center of the table, press 2¾″ wire nails up from the bottom through the table top, about ⅛″ from the edge. Bend the edges of the net over and over, forming a casing. Slip this down over the nails.

The paddles are simply cut from ¹⁄₁₆″ wood according to the pattern given. The handles are wrapped with tape or beading wire, and the faces are then painted with acrylic paint, one pair blue and one pair red, or faced with very thin rubber cut to fit.

The legs of the table are formed from ⅛″ hollow tubing, brass or aluminum, which is found in the miniature-railroad department of your hobby store. Cut two pieces 7½″ long. Then divide or mark ½″ from each end of each piece. Using your pliers, bend over at a right angle. Bend again at the 2½″ mark. Do this at both ends of the pieces of tubing. The ½″ ends are for attaching to the reinforcements underneath the table; tap these flat with your hammer, and then force ⅝″ wire nails through them and into the table. Repeat with the other leg formation. You're ready to serve!

Dart Board

A regulation dart board is a circle with an adult-size diameter of 18″, or 1½″ in our scale. Here we will use the exact scale, or perhaps even enlarge it a bit, since we want the board to show up well against the bamboo wallpaper.

Cut a circle with a diameter of 2″ from the cork scraps left from your floor. With a pencil, mark a circle with a diameter of 1½″ in the exact center. Spread the inner circle thinly with glue.

Now, using ⅛″ quilling paper, in the exact center fasten the paper around a pin and stick into the center mark. Gradually wrap the quilling paper around and around, pressing against the cork background and perhaps holding with a dab of glue every so often until the entire 1½″ circle in the center is filled. Cut off. (This is the way all good dart boards are made, so that the darts will stick in them readily.) You might draw the board facing using the model shown, or cut a diagram of a facing from one of the mail-order catalogues. Cut, and glue against the board. The board itself may be mounted on a square of the cork material for hanging; this makes it a great deal more impressive.

Billiard Table

The billiard table, designed by Charles W. Betty of Webster Groves, Missouri, a winner in the 1975 Originality Contest sponsored by *Dollhouse and Miniature News,* is easy to make from Mr. Betty's detailed plans.

Materials Needed for This Project
Masonite scraps
Solid walnut scraps
1 small square "Flan" self-stick green flannel (Woolworth's)
1 small piece venetian-blind cord

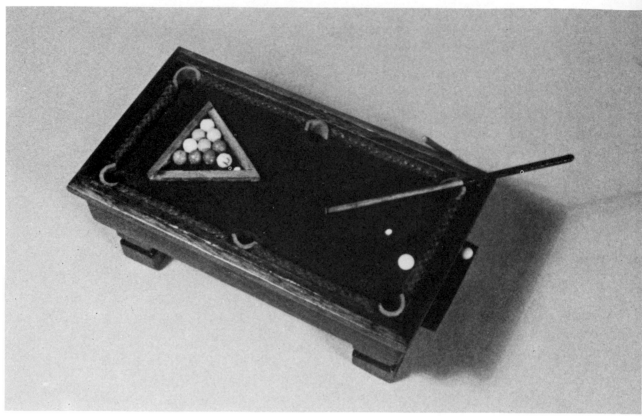

The billiard table, for which instructions are provided, was executed by Charles W. Betty.

1 small piece 1″ garden hose, split
1 empty beer can
  Gun pellets or beads
1 length ⅛″ dowel, 12″ long
  Stain and varnish
  Liquid hide glue
  Assorted paint for balls and cue ends
  Leather scrap

All pieces, as always, must be cut, stained, and finished before proceeding. Of the two pieces of masonite, one will be the top. On this, mount the piece of self-stick green flannel. Cut the ball trough from a flattened-out beer can to fit the masonite pieces. Elevate one end of the metal opposite the ball return by gluing a piece of ¼″ wood on the underneath. Turn up the edges at the end (A) for the ball return. Glue the top piece of masonite against the edges of the apron pieces, making butt joints on the apron. The top should be depressed enough to accommodate the cord trim around the edge.

Figure 47
Billiard Table

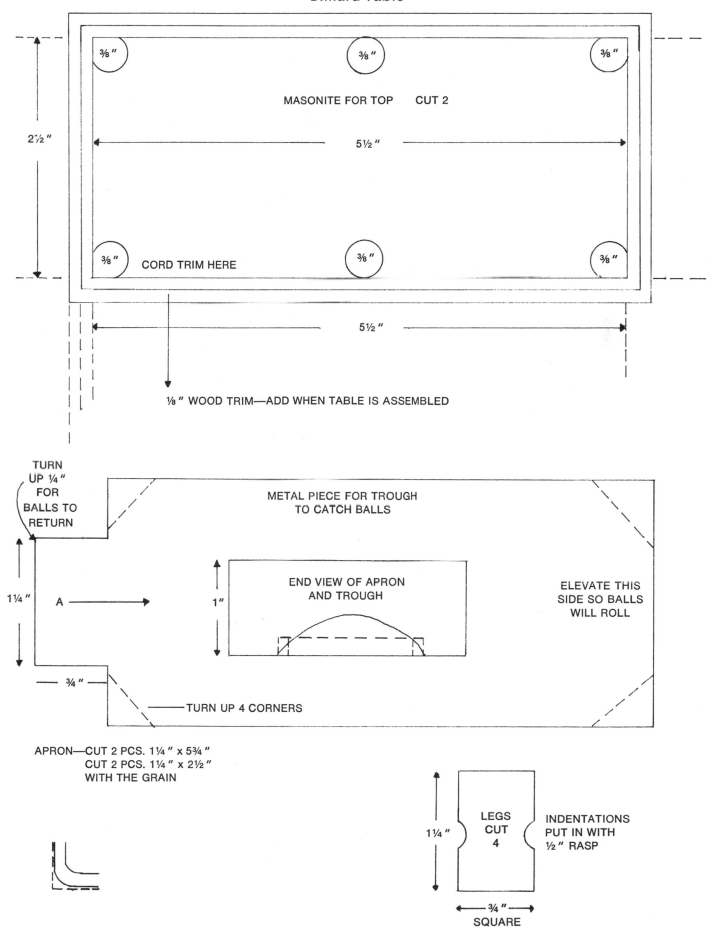

⅜ " ⅜ " ⅜ "

MASONITE FOR TOP   CUT 2

2½ "

5½ "

⅜ " CORD TRIM HERE ⅜ " ⅜ "

5½ "

↓ ⅛ " WOOD TRIM—ADD WHEN TABLE IS ASSEMBLED

TURN
UP ¼ "
FOR
BALLS TO
RETURN

METAL PIECE FOR TROUGH
TO CATCH BALLS

ELEVATE THIS
SIDE SO BALLS
WILL ROLL

1¼ "   A ⟶

1"   END VIEW OF APRON
AND TROUGH

¾ "

TURN UP 4 CORNERS

APRON—CUT 2 PCS. 1¼ " x 5¾ "
       CUT 2 PCS. 1¼ " x 2½ "
       WITH THE GRAIN

1¼ "   LEGS
        CUT
        4

INDENTATIONS
PUT IN WITH
½ " RASP

¾ "
SQUARE

Glue the metal trough (with one end elevated) against the bottom piece of masonite; then fit this bottom piece against the apron also, making butt joints. Notice that in one end piece of the apron an opening has been cut to accommodate the metal where the balls will roll. Attach the four legs to the bottom, just inside the apron, and glue pieces of $\frac{1}{8}''$ wood $\frac{1}{4}''$ wide, between them for support.

Paint the venetian-blind cord a billiard green and glue along the edges between the pockets. Fit the garden hose into the pockets and glue. Glue a tiny white dot ($\frac{1}{16}''$ diameter) in the center of the table $1\frac{7}{8}''$ from one end and $\frac{5}{8}''$ from the other end.

Gun pellets or beads are painted to resemble balls—don't forget the eight-ball! Cues are made from $\frac{1}{8}''$ dowels, $4\frac{1}{8}''$ long. The dowels are stained and the handles finished with dark brown enamel $1\frac{7}{8}''$ up from the end. Don't forget the tiny tip of leather that Mr. Betty was so careful to add!

17 Crèche

Since the crèche was one of the earliest of miniature rooms—it has been ascribed by some historians as being the beginning of the miniature-room idea—and because it is the very essence of simplicity, it seems only fitting to end this book with the creation of a room that represents a beginning to many of the world's peoples.

If you do a little research, a crèche can be made in the manner of any country in the world. You can do it in dull colors to represent the irony of Mary and Joseph being denied a room at the inn, or you can do it in strong, vibrant colors to carry the feeling that this was the beginning of a whole new life.

I decided to do mine using only natural materials and in the manner of stable, a style that will be easy for any beginner.

Look for twigs. The corner posts in this crèche were 1″ twigs or branches. The horizontal supports were ½″ twigs. The back of the stable was composed of stalks from a growth of pampas grass in my meadow, cut after it had dried. Where actual wood was used, it is the roughest sort, from a lettuce crate; but finding such crates may give you the most trouble since most vegetables are now shipped in corrugated boxes.

Materials Needed for This Project

1 length ¼″ wood, 18″ × 8″, for base
2 lengths ¼″ strips, ½″ wide and 8″ long
   Very rough wood, ⅛″ or ¼″ thick, in widths from 1″ to ¼″
6 1″ branches
6 ½″ twigs
   Twigs to finish top front
   Tacks
   Tacky glue or liquid hide glue
   Sphagnum moss

An Old World crèche made from twigs has figures that were hand carved by an ancestor of the Mallon family of St. Louis and brought here from Frankfurt in 1830. The colors are very bright still, and the paint seems to be homemade with natural coloring. Notice that someone at a later date has marked bricks on the manger.

Prepare the base by tacking the two ½"-wide strips of ¼" wood to the sides of the base (in this case 8") to set the stable up off the stand.

Cut the twigs to measure. Against the two back posts, tack strips of ¼" wood cut to fit to strengthen the wall. Glue, then tack, the posts at front as shown in the illustration about 1" back from the edge of the base. Attach the side twigs first, since after the posts are erected, they won't take any hammering.

Cut the pieces of pampas grass to fit; then tack or glue against the back crosspiece, which is 1" wide and ¼" thick. On the reverse side, support by gluing another piece of wood ½" wide and ¼" thick. Tack supporting pieces at top and bottom. I used sphagnum moss in various

A back view of the crèche shows construction detail. Stalks forming the back wall just happened to be on hand. Any natural stalk would do for the back wall and roof.

shades of green and brown (from your hobby shop in the HO department) for the roof and floor.

To make the roof, cut more strips of ½″-wide wood to fit the angle at the front and back. Glue in a 1″ branch that has been cut to fit the angle, from front to back. Glue in supporting pieces at the top of the posts at the sides. Then glue on more stalks from front to back.

Be sure to keep it rough. I used brown stain on the floor but left the back natural. Notice that I have used dimensions here that make it possible to build a diorama background similar to the one that is described in Chapter 15. I used a scene typical of Bethlehem and set it in a box of the dimensions of all my boxes. This makes it possible to slip the crèche into the box for display and remove it when I desire to use the crèche alone for a Christmas decoration.

You may not be lucky enough to have inherited quaint hand-carved pieces such as are shown in the photo, but perhaps you could carve a set to become an heirloom for your own family!

Shalom!

Figure 48
Creche
In 1/2 of 1/12 Scale

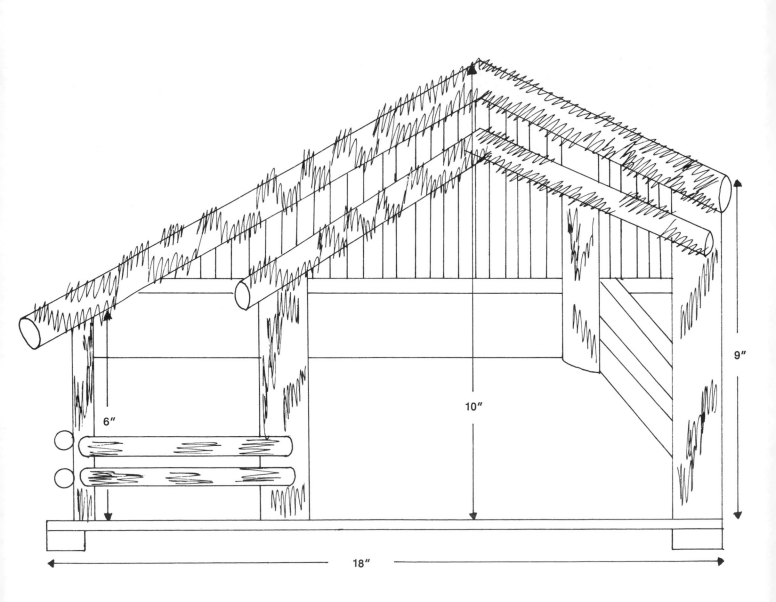

9"

10"

6"

18"

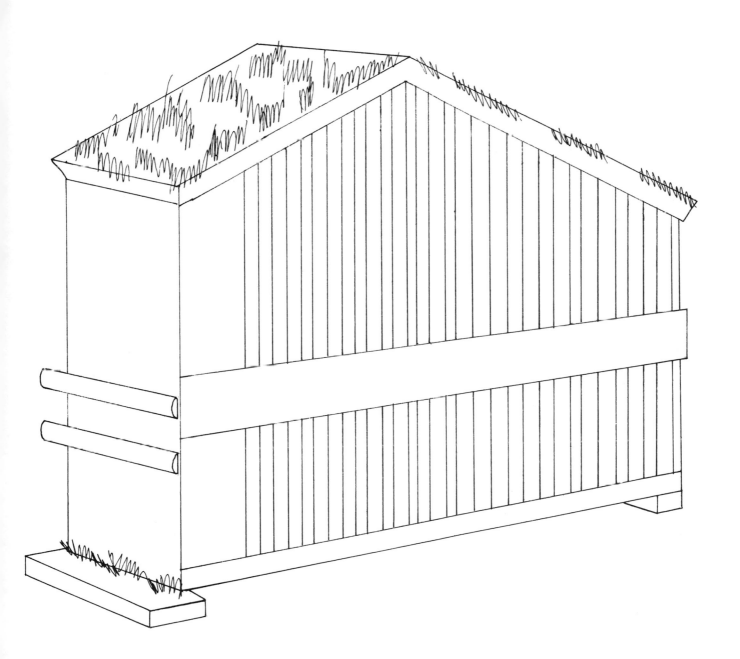

Appendix: List of Suppliers for Miniature-Room Building and Furnishing

Amity Petites
P.O. Box 2882
Lancaster, Calif. 93534

Real oak floors made to order. Write for details on other miniatures.

Architectural Model Supplies, Inc.
P.O. Box 3497, 115b Bellam Blvd.
San Rafael, Calif. 94902

Figures, millwork, garden pieces, everything you need. Send $1.50 for catalogue.

Earl J. Bccsc
Rt. 1, Box 777
Antioch, Ill. 60002

Solid-wood louvered shutters made to your order or standard window size.

Charles Bergeron
123 Laurel Ave.
Bradford, Mass. 01830

Send 50¢ for list of moldings and floorings. All sorts, hand turned.

Dick Blick, Art Supplies
P.O. Box 1267
Galesburg, Ill. 61401

Every art supply you might need, many indispensable aids for building.

Borrower's Press
Jane Bernier
Rt. 1
Winterport, Maine 04496

Handmade books for your library. Send SASE* for list.

Molly Brody, Miniatures
20 Sunset Hill Ave.,
Norwalk, Conn. 06851

Dolls, miniature furniture, fireplaces, many special pieces. Send $1.50 for catalogue.

Kathleen Buffum
42 Llanberris Rd.
Bala-Cynwyd, Pa. 19004

Fine oil paintings for mini rooms—portraits, scenes. Write for suggestions.

Burnett Fine Art Studio
2161 S. Dallas St.
Denver, Colo. 80231

Museum-type paintings, usually portraits, by an internationally known artist. Write for information.

Carlson's Miniatures
1S761 Bender Lane
West Chicago, Ill. 60185

Fine miniature rooms and miniatures. Panel doors, windows that work, any hand-finished millwork.

Chestnut Hill Studio
P.O. Box 38
Churchville, N.Y. 14428

Send $3.00 for catalogue that includes doors, windows, and paneling in exquisite detail.

Constantine's
2050 Eastchester Rd.
Bronx, N.Y. 10461

Big catalogue lists wide range of woods, veneers, many tools, and molded decorations.

Craft Patterns & Craft Products
Elmhurst, Ill. 60126

Send $1.00 for catalogue of dollhouses, mini rooms, plus kits for these and furniture.

Craftsman Wood Service
2727 Mary St.
Chicago, Ill. 60608

Send for catalogue listing tools, veneers, all woods, paints, and finishes.

Creative Craft House
910 St. Vincent Ave.
Santa Barbara, Calif. 93101

Send $1.00 for catalogue listing many things for mini rooms and houses, nicely illustrated.

Dollhouse Factory
P.O. Box 456, 157 Main St.
Lebanon, N.J. 08833

Dollhouses to order and build, building hardware, stained glass. Send $1.00 for catalogue.

Dollhouse Factory
P.O. Box 2232
Sunnyvale, Calif. 94087

Send $1.00 for catalogue, featuring furniture and accessories, mostly for 12" dolls. Also wallpaper.

Dollhouses
Louis and Barbara Kummerow
16460 Wagon Wheel Dr.
Riverside, Calif. 92506

Send SASE* for catalogue of ¼" to 1" ideas, glass, mirrors, many accessories.

Dolls' Cobbler
Sylvia Rountree
1930 Falls Ave.
Cuyahoga Falls, Ohio 44223

Slippers, boots, saddles, many accessories expertly made.

Dolphin Originals
Bob Bernhard
7302 Hasbrook Ave.
Philadelphia, Pa. 19111

Dollhouses and miniature rooms to order, fine furniture in miniature. Send $1.00 for list. 50¢ for photos.

Madeline Gesser
Interior Decorator
221 Everit Ave.
Hewlett Harbor, N.Y. 11557

Magnificent contemporary pieces of lucite and walnut; many miniature accessories. Write for prices and information.

Glassblower's Workshop
1212 S. Coast Highway
Laguna Beach, Calif. 92651

Send $1.00 for catalogue showing unbelievable list of hand-blown glass items in miniature.

Green Door Studio
517 E. Annapolis St.
St. Paul, Minn. 55118

Patterns for almost anything in miniatures from houses to wheelbarrows. Send 50¢.

Harold's Handcrafted Instruments
21901 Harding
Oak Park, Mich. 48237

Send 10¢ for list of fine musical instruments and miniatures.

Joe Hermes
P.O. Box 23
El Monte, Calif. 91734

Send SASE* for list. Wallpapers, glues, some miniature pieces.

Holgate & Raynolds
601 Davis St.
Evanston, Ill. 60201

Send $1.00 for catalogue, which includes HO and many plastic surfaces, metal minis.

Illinois Hobbycraft 12 S. Fifth St. Geneva, Ill. 60134	Send $1.00 for comprehensive catalogue of lighting equipment, construction materials, and tools.
It's a Small World 542 Lincoln Ave. Winnetka, Ill. 60093	Send $2.00 for catalogue. One-of-a-kind pieces only. Write advising your needs.
Joen Ellen Kanze 26 Palmer Ave. North White Plains, N.Y. 10603	Dollhouses built to order, many supplies, handmade things. Send $1.00 for list.
Maid of Scandinavia 3244 Raleigh Ave. Minneapolis, Minn. 55416	Supply house for home bakers; lists many things mini size that can be used in rooms or dollhouses. $1.00 for catalogue.
Make It Happen Craft Studio 2620B West Chester Pike Broomall, Pa. 19008	Write advising your needs. Many findings and supplies for furniture, lighting, etc.
Miniature Mart 883 - 39th Ave. San Francisco, Calif. 94121	Light fixtures, dishes, moldings, wallpapers, hinges, dinnerware, and furniture. Send $2.00 for catalogue.
C. A. ("Chuck") Newland 2465 E. Commonwealth Ave. Fullerton, Calif. 92631	Builds dollhouses to order; offers large variety of lumber and corner trim. Send SASE* for list.
Norm Nielsen 6678 S. Clayton St. Littleton, Colo. 80121	Miniature rooms, dollhouses, lumber for building. Write your wants.
Northeastern Scale Models, Inc. P.O. Box 425 Methuen, Mass. 01844	Send $1.50 for catalogue of patterns, moldings, and woods. Also flooring, siding, and many ideas.
Pendragon House, Inc. 899 Broadway Ave. Redwood City, Calif. 94063	Charming booklet printed in England showing rooms in Victoria and Albert Museum. Write for price.
Pink Sleigh P.O. Box 35 Oldwick, N.J. 08858	Interesting list of many small pieces: beads, jewelry findings, many others.
Pamela Schoenborn 3–9 Daita 6-chome Setagaya-Ku, Tokyo 155, Japan	Antiques and new minis from Japan and Asia. Send $1.50 for catalogue of miniature Japanalia.
Doreen Sinnett Designs 418 Santa Ana Ave. Newport Beach, Calif. 92660	Mini rooms, doll houses, supplies for making bricks and shingles, many others. Send $1.00 for catalogue.
Emil and Lucy Spinka 519 Selborne Rd. Riverside, Ill. 60546	Finest of miniatures from catalogue or made to order. Send $2.00 for catalogue.
The Workshop Howard Pierce 424 N. Broadview Wichita, Kans. 67208	Fireplaces, many fine copies of old pieces, store fixtures, windows, doors, moldings. Catalogue $1.00.

* Self-addressed stamped envelope.

Index